# Voices From Beyond

## Victor S. Mannahan, CPI

In Cooperation With:

www.silverstateparanormal.org

# Voices From Beyond

## Scott Mannahan, CPI

© 2011 Victor S. Mannahan
All Rights Reserved
ISBN 978-1-105-26871-7

# ACKNOWLEDGMENTS

I would like to take this opportunity to thank those who have helped me in my paranormal travels. Without them, I would never have had the opportunity to discover what lies beyond. To **Gerre Young**, thanks for all the pats on the back, and the countless times you have stood up for me, and what I believe in. To **Jill Smith**, whose positive attitude always made me feel welcome, thanks for making me feel like I was always your #1 guy. To **Petra Bradt**, thanks for taking me in as your lead tech. I learned a great deal, and really enjoyed those cold nights with you and the posse at Bower's Mansion.

To my neighbor **Boe Smith**, who showed me the best evidence of life after death I have ever seen. I thank you for trusting such a unique discovery to me, and for tagging along during those long, cold nights at the Dayton Cemetery. To **my family,** I also thank you for enduring my sometimes bizarre obsession with the afterlife, and for allowing hoards of strangers from different paranormal teams to use your home as a rest stop. I would also like to thank the **citizens and business owners of Virginia City, Nevada** for all their hospitality, and for allowing me to investigate some of the most haunted locations I have ever visited. Thanks to **Ghost Adventures,** for giving me the opportunity to investigate the Goldfield Hotel during the 2008 live ghost hunt. It has forever changed my opinion of what lies beyond, and I frequently dream of going back again. While I know I might be preaching to deaf ears here, I also just want to say thanks to all the **spirits of those who I have investigated. May they all rest in peace.**

# PARANORMAL INVESTIGATOR'S OATH

NEVER PROVIDE OR ENDORSE FALSE EVIDENCE OR TESTIMONY

NEVER EXPLOIT THE PARANORMAL FOR PERSONAL GAIN

UNLESS USING THE FUNDS TO EDUCATE, GIVE BACK TO THE COMMUNITY, OR FINANCE FURTHER STUDY, NEVER USE THE PARANORMAL FOR MONETARY GAIN

ALWAYS REPRESENT THE CLIENT, AND GLOBAL PARANORMAL COMMUNITY HONESTLY AND ETHICALLY

RESPECT THE ENVIRONMENT AND THE POTENTIAL SPIRITS BEING INVESTIGATED

NEVER ALLOW PERSONAL BELIEF TO INFLUENCE EVIDENCE COLLECTION OR REVIEW

KEEP AN OPEN MIND, AND REMAIN AVAILABLE TO OTHER IDEAS AND TECHNIQUES

ENCOURAGE COOPERATION WITH OTHER INVESTIGATORS, NOT COMPETETION

 CONTENTS

**VI  INTRODUCTION TO PARANORMAL INVESTIGATION AND EVP**

**9  CHAPTER ONE:** History of Electronic Voice Phenomena

**17  CHAPTER TWO:** EVP & AVP Classifications

**21  CHAPTER THREE:** Tools Of The Trade

**41  CHAPTER FOUR:** Recording Techniques & Guidelines

**66  CHAPTER FIVE:** Reviewing Your Evidence

**77  CHAPTER SIX:** Understanding Sound Analysis

**87  CONCLUSION**

**89  GLOSSARY OF TERMS**

# INTRODUCTION
## Ghost Hunting & EVP's

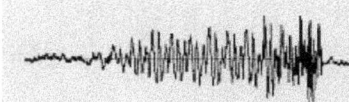

You will notice in the heading above, that I used the term "Ghost Hunting". I used this to bring up an important point; I am not a Ghost Hunter. I think this is a term used to try and promote oneself, or to make what a person does in this field look more exotic or important. The term seems to be getting used more and more these days, and most teams do not truly understand how using it makes them look. I think the term creates a very negative and uneducated picture of the paranormal. I do not hunt ghosts, I investigate them. I have the utmost respect for the spirits I encounter, and I personally do not think calling myself a "Hunter of Ghosts" or "Finder of Ghosts" will grant me any favors when it comes to evidence gathering. I also do not think it will attract legitimate clients with real problems either.

Often, I see other teams labeling themselves in this manner, and putting this information for the entire world to read on their shirts, business cards, and personal vehicles. These teams will walk into an investigation, and introduce themselves to the potential spirits they are investigating as ghost hunters, but at the same time inform them they are not there to harm them. What is wrong with this picture? This is like going deer hunting, and telling the deer you are not going to hurt them, but at the same time wearing a deer hunting patch, and pointing your hunting rifle at them.

We are not "Ghost Hunters"; we are "Paranormal Investigators" or "Truth Seekers". I am not saying that all investigators who use this term are weekend warriors, and I know some really good investigators who call themselves ghost hunters. However, from my experience, the most reputable investigators tend to be the ones who take a more humble approach when it comes to personal representation. So, before you describe yourself as a ghost hunter, ask yourself if <u>you</u> would like to be hunted. Ask yourself what type of investigator <u>you</u> seem like to a potential spirit, and your client.

Do you also imagine yourself in a tan jumpsuit with a proton pack strapped to your back? The perceptions that most people have when it comes to paranormal investigation, are often glamorized by television shows and motion pictures. The truth actually paints a far different picture. The paranormal requires patience, dedication, lots of funding and a large investigative team to investigate properly. Paranormal investigation while exciting at times, is actually quite tedious and boring. I love to investigate and walk through old, historic buildings. I also enjoy meeting new people who have unique ghost stories to tell, and most of all, helping those in need. These are all fun and exciting, however, what most people fail to see behind the scenes are the countless hours of listening to audio. Hours of watching, and scrutinizing photos and video sessions. Researching historical records and blueprints, interviewing clients and their neighbors, raising funds for equipment and travel expenses. Interviewing and recruiting new team members, coping with the inevitable drama that occurs from having friends and family on the same team, while dealing with the endless amount of skepticism from those who refuse to believe. The list seems to go on forever, and can be a frustrating one.

For those of you who have experience in paranormal investigation, you will already know what it takes to be proficient in this field of study, and you know the sacrifices that have to be made. You also know that the paranormal requires constant learning. The purpose of this book, however redundant it may seem to veteran investigators, is to educate investigators just starting out who wish to learn. This book is going to focus on some of the basic principles of investigation when it comes to audio capture, and something every single investigator should be familiar with and prepare for; voices from beyond, or EVP. It does not matter what type of investigator you are, how often you investigate, or what your skill level resides at, and chances are, nearly 90% of you have experienced a mysterious voice in your recordings. I do not claim to be an expert when it comes to EVP, or a professional writer, for that matter, but I often get asked how one starts to record these mysterious voices, which is why I decided to write this book.

This book, while mainly for the rookie investigator, is also for the experienced as well. If you study the paranormal, you have to keep learning, and this includes all aspects of evidence you might obtain, especially EVP. Audio is the most common type of paranormal evidence reported today, and therefore, it should be studied the most.

If you are ignoring these mysterious voices, and dismissing them simply because you are unable to understand them, or because some skeptic is suggesting they are just random radio waves, then shame on you! Furthermore, if you are assuming that just because there is a voice on your recording that should not be there, that it is automatically a spirit voice, then shame on you for that too! The first thing you have to do is examine all the evidence, and then decide how you feel about the audio you have captured. Never let anybody make up your mind for you or tell you how you should feel when it comes to the evidence you collect. You should always be your only critic, and remember that your personal beliefs will directly affect how you interpret your evidence! As a paranormal investigator, the number one weapon in your arsenal is an open mind, and I encourage you to keep it open!

Actual Intelligent Spirit Capture

**Photo courtesy of Boe Smith**

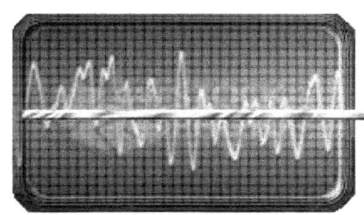

# ~ CHAPTER ONE ~
## THE HISTORY OF EVP

### AM I ALLOWED TO SAY "PARANORMAL"? IS EVP TABOO?

Before we can comprehend what exactly is involved in capturing and analyzing EVP, first I think it would better to understand what they are, and how these mysterious voices first came to the attention of paranormal investigators. For those of you unfamiliar with the term, EVP stands for **Electronic Voice Phenomena.** Simply put, they are disembodied voices and sounds captured on different types of recording equipment and media. In the world of paranormal evidence, EVP rules supreme. This is largely because they are the number one form of legitimate reported paranormal evidence, and the easiest to obtain.

Yes, I did say, Paranormal. We can say it now right? We are all adults, are we not? Most investigators are reluctant to associate any evidence they obtain with the paranormal in fear that some skeptic is going to discredit their evidence, and make them look foolish. In my opinion, over half of these anomalous sounds can usually be explained as just residual energy or common noises. The other half are the genuine article, and proving that they are genuine is no easy task. Sure, it can be classified as an EVP, but is it an authentic spirit voice? Let us not forget they are two completely different things! All we can honestly conclude, is they are "Paranormal" in nature; a word that many investigators have seemed to ignore the definition of over recent years.

The word **"Paranormal"** by definition simply means out of the realm of scientific explanation. When a sound or voice is captured that should not be there to begin with, and when all other possible explanations have been exhausted as to its existence, then obviously it should be labeled paranormal in nature, until a scientific explanation can be found in the future.

Do not be afraid to classify any evidence you may obtain as paranormal, and do not automatically assume that just because it is paranormal, that it is automatically a spirit voice. It is the same as seeing a UFO in the night sky. Just because you label something a UFO, does not mean that it is an alien spacecraft. It simply means that you saw an object which was flying, that for various reasons, you could not identify. If it cannot be identified, then it is not a confirmed alien spacecraft. I guess my point, here is simple; never be reluctant to use the term Paranormal. It may sound extravagant, overly technical, and give you visions of ghostly apparitions when you think of it, but it is after all just a term that is used to classify the events investigators need to catalog.

## A LONG MYSTERIOUS HISTORY

How long has Electronic Voice Phenomena been around, and how was it first discovered? Well, EVP has been around since man has been able to record sound. The first practical, sound recording and reproduction device was called the **Mechanical Phonograph Cylinder** invented by Thomas Edison in 1877, and later patented in 1878. Commonly known as "records" in their era of popularity (1888–1915), these cylinder shaped objects had an audio recording engraved on the outer waxy surface which could be reproduced when the cylinder was rotated and played on a mechanical phonograph.

As the Spiritualism Movement became popular in the 1840s–1920s, with a belief that the spirits of the dead could be contacted by mediums, new technologies of the era, including photography were used by spiritualists in an effort to make contact with a spirit world. So popular were such ideas, that Thomas Edison was asked in an interview with *Scientific American* to comment on the possibility of using his inventions to communicate with spirits. He replied that if the spirits were only capable of subtle influences, a sensitive audio recording device would provide a better chance of spirit communication than the traditional techniques of the time. As sound recording became widespread, mediums explored using this technology to establish communication with the dead as well. Spiritualism declined in the latter part of the 20th century, but attempts to use portable recording devices, and modern digital technologies to communicate with spirits grew in popularity.

American photographer Attila Von Szalay was among the first to try recording what he believed to be voices of the dead. He began his attempts in 1941 using a 78 rpm record, but it was not until 1956, after switching to a reel-to-reel magnetic tape recorder, that he was successful. Working with Raymond Bayless, Von Szalay conducted a number of recording sessions with a custom-made apparatus, consisting of a microphone in an insulated cabinet connected to an external recording device and speaker.

Attila von Szalay

Szalay reported finding many sounds on the tape that could not be heard on the speaker at the time of recording, some of which were recorded when there was no one in the cabinet. He believed these sounds to be the voices of discarnate spirits. Among the first recordings believed to be spirit voices were such messages as "This is G!", "Hot dog, Art!", and "Merry Christmas and Happy New Year to you all" and their work was published by the Journal of the American Society for Psychical Research in 1959. Bayless later went on to co-author the 1979 book, Phone Calls from the Dead.

In 1959, Swedish painter and film producer Friedrich Jürgenson was recording bird songs. Upon playing the tape later, he heard what he interpreted to be his late father's voice, and then the spirit of his deceased wife calling his name. He went on to make several more recordings, including one that he said contained a message from his late mother.

Friedrich Jurgenson

Konstantin Raudive, a Latvian psychologist who had taught at the University of Uppsala, Sweden and who had personally worked with Jürgenson, made over 100,000 recordings, which he described, as being communications with discarnate people.

Some of these recordings were conducted in an RF (radio frequency) screened laboratory, and contained words Raudive said were distinct and perfectly understandable. In an attempt to validate the content of his collection of recordings, Raudive invited listeners to hear and interpret them with notable success, which eventually led to various other experiments involving **Audible Matrixing** or **Pareidolia**, which I will explain in later chapters. He believed that the clarity of the voices heard in his recordings implied that they could not be readily explained by rational means, thus categorizing them later as paranormal. Raudive published his first book, ***Breakthrough: An Amazing Experiment in Electronic Communication with the Dead*** in 1968 and translated into English in 1971, and I highly recommend it as a tool of study for all paranormal enthusiasts.

Konstantin Raudive

## Modern Interest

In 1982, Sarah Estep founded the American Association of Electronic Voice Phenomena (AAEVP), a nonprofit organization with the purpose of increasing awareness of EVP, and teaching standardized methods for capturing it. Estep began her exploration of EVP in 1976, and claims she has made hundreds of recordings including messages from deceased friends, relatives, and other individuals, including Konstantin Raudive, Beethoven, a lamplighter from 18th century Pennsylvania, and extraterrestrials whom she speculated originated from other planets.

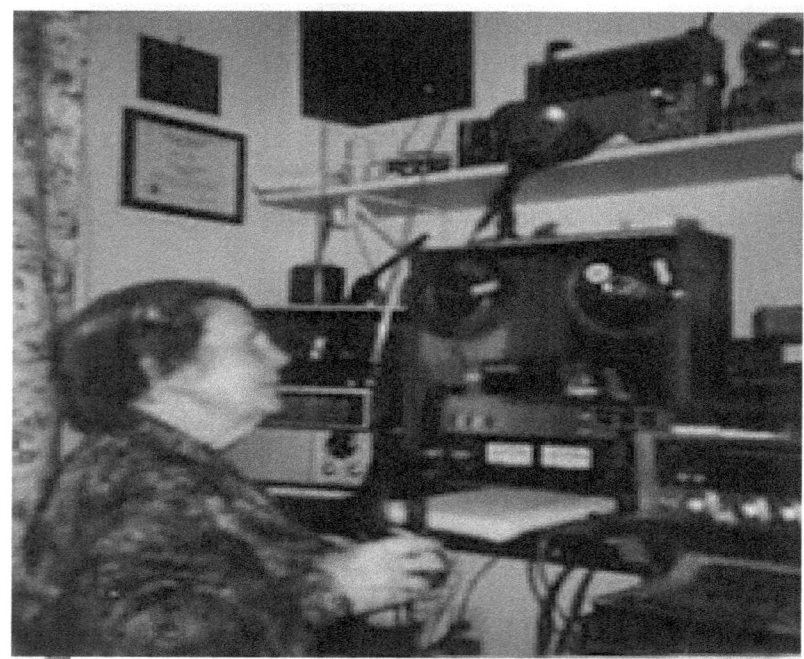

Sarah Estep
Founder Of The AAEVP

The term **Instrumental Trans-Communication (ITC)** was coined by Ernst Senkowski in the 1970's, and refers to communication through any sort of electronic device such as tape recorders, fax machines, television sets or computers between spirits. One particularly famous event of ITC occurred when the image of EVP enthusiast Friedrich Jürgenson (whose funeral was held that day) was said to have appeared on a television in the home of a colleague, which had been purposefully tuned to a vacant channel.

Ernst Senkowski – The Father Of ITC

In 1997, Imants Barušs, of the Department of Psychology at the University of Western Ontario, conducted a series of experiments using the methods of EVP investigator Konstantin Raudive, and the work of "Instrumental Transcommunication Researcher" Mark Macy, as a guide. A radio was tuned to an empty frequency, and a total of 60 hours and 11 minutes of recordings were collected. During recordings, a person either sat in silence or attempted to make verbal contact with potential sources of EVP. Barušs stated that he recorded several events that sounded like voices, but they were too few and too random to represent viable data. He concluded: "While we did replicate EVP in the weak sense, none of the phenomena found in our study was clearly anomalous, let alone attributable to discarnate beings. Hence we have failed to replicate EVP in the strong sense." The findings were published in the Journal of Scientific Exploration in 2001, and include a literature review.

In 1997, Imants Barušs, of the Department of Psychology at the University of Western Ontario, conducted a series of experiments using the methods of EVP investigator Konstantin Raudive, and the work of "instrumental transcommunication researcher" Mark Macy, as a guide. A radio was tuned to an empty frequency, and a total of 60 hours and 11 minutes of recordings were collected. During recordings, a person either sat in silence or attempted to make verbal contact with potential sources of EVP. Barušs stated that he did record several events that sounded like voices, but they were too few and too random to represent viable data. He concluded: "While we did replicate EVP in the weak sense, none of the phenomena found in our study was clearly anomalous, let alone attributable to discarnate beings. Hence we have failed to replicate EVP in the strong sense." The findings were published in the Journal of Scientific Exploration in 2001.

In recent years, with the growing popularity of paranormal television shows, there has been a new classification of anomalous sounds to hit the paranormal community, which are called AVP or **Audible Voice Phenomena.** Simply put, these are disembodied voices or sounds heard by investigators in the investigative environment at the time of investigation, and captured on at least one recording device. This type of audio, though very rare, is often the most undisputed of all, and is frequently associated with an intelligent spirit. I have personally heard these phenomena and experienced them for myself. It is an extremely humbling experience hearing a voice come out of thin air, and confirming the event by capturing it on audio is even more surreal.

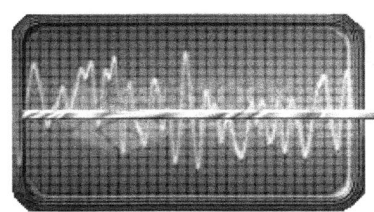

# ~ CHAPTER TWO ~
## EVP & AVP CLASSIFICATIONS

EVP comes in a wide variety of range and styles. Some are extremely strong and easy to discern, while others are remarkably subtle, and require some form of amplification or filtering to hear.

While there may be various reasons, including environmental, as to why they come in such a wide range of styles, investigators have come up with a classification system to measure the quality of EVP in an effort to help better understand and categorize them.

Many investigators come up with different classification systems to suit their individual tastes, and sometimes these might be different from group to group. The typical classifications consist of a short list of differences, but I personally do not agree with this. I have also concluded from my own personal experiences, that AVP also needs to have classifications as well. This is something most investigators completely overlook. Just because it is an audible voice, does not mean that it should not also be broken down and classified for further study. Like EVP, AVP also comes in a wide variety of styles and levels of clarity. Please keep in mind that paranormal research is typically an experimental science. There are no formal rules to follow on how to obtain and classify the potential evidence we gather, and therefore, a lot becomes theory and personal preference. This is my personal list of classifications, and while you may not agree with them, they are what work best for me.

# EVP Classifications

**Class A** - This is a class of EVP that are exceptionally loud and clear, and the rarest to obtain. They are easy to understand without having to guess what is being said. They require absolutely no digital enhancements of any form or amplification, nor do they usually require the use of headphones. These types of EVP are often associated with AVP as well, because of the superior clarity and strength of the recordings, especially if recorded on more than one recording device at the same time. EVP in this class are typically recorded at a frequency below or above the normal human speaking range. To protect the integrity of these types of recordings, they should NEVER be digitally enhanced or altered in any way.

**Class B** – This is the most common form of EVP. They are typically strong, but not quite as strong as a class A. They require subtle levels of digital enhancement. Typically, the voices are not clear enough and often there is a dispute as to what is being said. This type of EVP normally requires the use of headphones to be heard properly. It is also common for residual sounds and voices to be recorded in this class. Typically, anomalies in this class are of the same volume levels when compared to each other. Often, words like "Yes" and "No" sound exactly the same from recording to recording, regardless of the sex of the voice. EVP in this class is also typically recorded at a frequency below and above the normal human speaking ranges.

**Class C** - These are among the lowest quality EVP. They need moderate amounts of digital amplification, usually at least 2 or 3 steps of enhancement. They require an extremely quiet environment with the use of headphones to be heard, and often only one or two words can be understood. These types of EVP's often create confusion when heard, and are seldom taken seriously by investigators.

**Class T** - "Trash". These are clips of audio that may resemble EVP but require so many enhancements that they are no longer usable.

# **AVP Classifications**

**It must be heard by at least one investigator at the time/moment of capture**

**It must be captured on at least one recording device, and acknowledged on the recording at the time of capture for validation**

**Class 1 -** Just like class A EVP, these are also extremely rare to obtain. These are extremely easy to understand, loud, and can easily be located in a certain part of the room or building, and are typically followed by EMF (Electro Magnetic Flux) or cold sensation in the immediate area. Typically, they are heard by multiple investigators at the same time. AVP in this category are often confirmed by comparing the recording to what the other investigators heard at the time. These should also never be enhanced or altered in order to maintain validation. AVP in this class usually tends to be of the **intelligent** variety.

**Class 2 –** This is the most common form of AVP. A class 2 has many of the same attributes as a class 1, except the audible is not as clear, and it is often disputed as to what was being said. Pinpointing the exact direction of the source of the audio is sometimes difficult. Usually, one investigator or two will hear the anomalies, while others in the room, even those next to the ones that heard it, will not. The voices or sounds are often at a low level just like a whisper, and will often require some level of digital enhancement in order to make them louder. AVP in this class usually tends to be both **intelligent** and **residual** varieties.

**Class 3 –** These are AVP that were heard and recorded, but are so garbled or faint, that it cannot be agreed as to what was heard. This type of AVP is often disregarded unless other evidence can be documented at the same time, which would lend validation to the event.

# **Types OF EVP & AVP**

While there are several classifications for EVP and AVP, they both fall into one of two groups:

**Residual** – Events trapped in time, which seem to repeat themselves over and over. These may be triggered by certain stimulus such as music, reenactments, and specific dates in time. These events can include EVP and AVP audio, as well as visual manifestations, but no intelligent evidence is usually associated with the activity.

**Intelligent –** Events that are unique to the specific situation. Often respond to direct questioning or stimulus, are predictable, and are associated with other events such as sudden temperature changes, EMF spikes, smells or odors, object manipulation, and visible manifestations. If the event makes significant, measurable changes to the environment, or directly responds to the investigator(s), chances are it falls into this class.

Please understand that these are my personal classifications, and you may have different ones, or you may know other teams that use other variations. These are not written in stone, and I urge you to use what works best for you. Perhaps one day when we know more about Electronic Voice Phenomena, these classifications will change and become universal, but until then, what you have read here is pretty much the standard. Just remember, that all voice phenomena, regardless of what category they may fall into, are worth your attention. Only by careful analysis can we actually decide which ones are genuine and which ones are not. Never ignore any potential evidence until you have fully analyzed it for yourself.

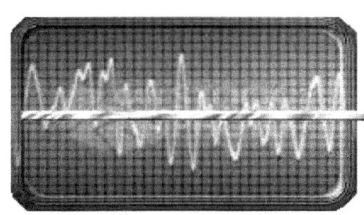

# ~ CHAPTER THREE ~
## TOOLS OF THE TRADE

As you can probably guess, the equipment that investigators use today is quite different from the equipment that was used at the emergence of audio recording. While a lot has changed from the days of Thomas Edison's Mechanical Phonograph Cylinder, some seemingly ancient technologies are still in use today. I have personally used many different types of recording equipment and various brands over the years, and there is a distinct difference in the quality of evidence you can obtain from one device to the next. Unfortunately, I personally believe you get what you pay for, and if you are looking for quality, it is going to cost you. I of course am not saying that you need to spend hundreds of dollars on a voice recorder or other recording equipment, as I have seen a $25 voice recorder capture decent evidence. I do, however, suggest spending a little extra and getting decent quality. I cannot even count how many times I have seen investigators purchase what they thought was a decent voice recorder, only to discover later that it did not have the features they required. It did not hook up to a computer, did not have enough internal memory to last the entire investigation, broke down after only a few months, and microphone sensitivity was horrid at best.

Besides a decent digital or full-spectrum camera, your voice recorder is perhaps the most important investment you will ever make when it comes to equipment, and you should not cut corners on quality or reliability to save a few bucks. In this chapter, I will discuss the various types of recorders used today, which ones I think are the best, which ones are not, and what features you need to look for when making a purchase. Worry not, you can get quality evidence for under $100, and some pretty sweet features also.

# MAGNETIC TAPE

Developed in Germany, **Magnetic tape** is a medium for magnetic recording, made of a thin magnetic coating on a long, narrow strip of plastic. Devices that record and play back audio or video using magnetic tape are called tape recorders and videotape recorders. A device that stores computer data on magnetic tape is a tape drive or tape unit streamer. Magnetic tape revolutionized broadcasting and recording. When all radio was live, it allowed programming to be prerecorded. At a time when gramophone records recorded in one take, it allowed recordings in multiple parts, which were mixed and edited with tolerable loss in quality.

It is a key technology in early computer development, allowing huge amounts of data to be mechanically created, stored for long periods and rapidly accessed. Today, other technologies have taken the place of magnetic tape, and a new digital world of audio/data capture has emerged. Despite this innovation in technology, tape is still widely used by many paranormal investigators today with excellent results, but not without a few drawbacks.

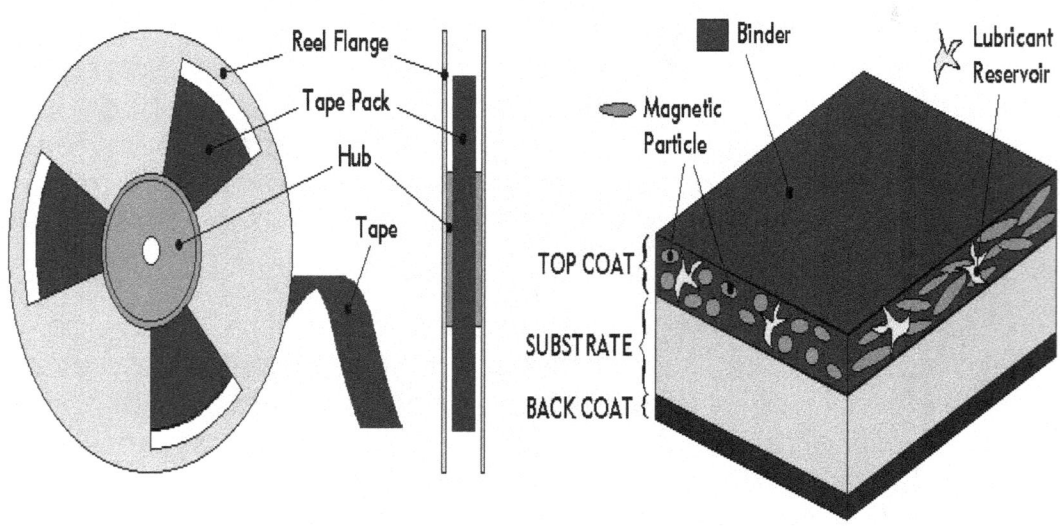

Magnetic tape recording devices, though redundant compared to newer technology, remain at the forefront of EVP research for some, and for several reasons. For starters, the audio is valid because it has not been digitally converted in a smaller file size, or other format. Another positive attribute that investigators claim, is the ability of internal noise from the moving parts, and the magnetic motors, to give the spirits a better method in which to communicate. Furthermore, since some of the first EVP ever captured were on magnetic tape, many investigators are reluctant to switch to anything different. While these are all valid reasons, I personally think that using this older technology poses far more risks than benefits, and I will explain why.

I have used magnetic tape on several occasions, and other investigators I have worked with in the past have also used it. Yes, a conventional solid-state magnetic tape recorder is hard to beat as far as reliability goes, and the audio is suitable from these older devices, but I still do not recommend that any investigator use them. It is acceptable, when it is not the only method of audio capture, and other methods are being used also, but to solely rely on it is extremely risky. Magnetic tape itself can be particularly problematic as far as storage and reliability go. Over time, magnetic tape can suffer from deterioration called **Sticky-Shed Syndrome**, caused by absorption of moisture into the binder of the tape, which can render the tape unusable.

Another thing to watch out for is stretching. When analyzing any audio, especially EVP, the investigator will be required to rewind and fast forward several times in order to make sense of any anomaly found on the recording. This over time, will eventually cause the tape to stretch out, causing slack, which of course can lead to many other problems. For those of you who are old enough, do you remember sitting in your bedroom in the 1970's and 80's? Remember using a pencil or ink pen to manually rewind your favorite audio cassette because your tape player's magnetic head reader became dirty and ate your tape? If you did not frequently use a special head cleaner in your Walkman, this would eventually happen, and it was very frustrating. I spent countless hours doing this when I was younger.

Another drawback to tape, is storage reliability. Magnetic tape over time, will eventually lose some of its magnetic coating, causing the audio to crackle, or not even be heard at all. Yes, it is true, this normally takes a very long time, but I have seen brand new quality tapes last only months before having to be thrown in the garbage can. There is also the matter of humidity, dust, and heat, which will all affect the longevity of your tape. I do not know about you, but I sure do not want to trust my important evidence to any of these factors. Ever accidentally leave your favorite music cassette on the dashboard of your car, only to come back after shopping to find that the magnetic tape inside the plastic case had melted together? Now, forget all the issues with storage, sound quality and longevity, and let us talk about something even more important; using old magnetic tape in combination with today's newer technologies.

So, you have your new mini tape recorder, and you are going to use it to investigate, which also means having to drive to the store and look for mini magnetic tape cassettes, which are getting harder and harder to find. After the investigation, you arrive home and discover that you may have a few EVP's on the recording, and you would like to enhance the audio, or view the frequencies you captured on your computer. Better yet, take out the individual audio clips, and email them to the rest of your team, or even post them on your web site. Problem; you cannot transfer them because the recorder is not USB or Serial Connection compatible.

Now, you are forced to transfer the audio into your computer by hooking up a cable between the recorder and your microphone port on your computer, having to press play on the recorder while audio software on your computer records it. Now, you are really in trouble! You are re-recording hours of audio just so you can get the files on your computer. Now, you have two recordings to worry about keeping track of instead of just one! In addition, let us not forget what happens to any audio stream when it is converted into another format; lossy audio! You are taking your potentially valuable evidence, and converting it from analog to digital, which defeats the purpose of recording on tape to begin with!

By the time you clean up, enhance, and snip your audio, you have taken so many steps that most investigators will no longer take your audio seriously. You have also recorded your original audio through the internal workings of your computer's sound card, which could have quite possibly picked up even more interference. You could have easily added even more anomalous sounds to your recording, or even worse, made those important EVP's harder to hear than before, requiring even more digital enhancement; a vicious circle! Sure, tape was the technology to have back 30 years ago, but with the advent of so many digital improvements, combining the two to be compatible with one another becomes more trouble than it is worth. If all you're looking to accomplish is to record EVP, leave them on tape forever, and never use them in any digital fashion, then I say go for it. However, if going the digital route, I highly suggest leaving magnetic tape right where it belongs; in the Stone Age! Some investigators like to use both technologies, and I encourage this if you are going to use tape. It certainly does not hurt to have both versions to compare.

Before I stray into the digital side of things, I also want to point out one more serious disadvantage about ANY magnetic tape recorder; frequency response. What we hear is ultimately dictated by the frequency response of our ears, and an audio recorder of any type, either analog or digital, is subject to the same law. Why does a dog hear things we cannot? Well, because a dog's hearing is designed to hear higher frequencies.

The same goes for different types of analog and digital recorders as well, because they are all made to cover different frequencies.

All tape recorders were originally designed for dictation purposes, and made to cover the typical human speaking range of 300-4000HZ (hertz). Try recording any music through one of these dictation recorders, and even with quality headphones, you will soon find out that the quality of the music is horrible compared to today's standards. This is because of the limited range in frequency response. What if an EVP was sent out by a spirit at a frequency of 15,000HZ? Your tape recorder would not even pick up the anomaly, because it did not cover that frequency, and you would have missed valuable evidence. As paranormal investigators, we need our recorders to hear as much of the human hearing range as possible! The normal human hearing range is from 20-20,000HZ. Just like our eyes should see 20/20, our ears should hear in the 20-20,000HZ range as well. In order to hear as much as possible in the investigative environment, we need a recorder that can hear as well as we do, if not better, so potential evidence is not missed.

Ever put on a low quality set of headphones, and then listen to a song, and then listen to the same song again with quality headphones? You hear sounds you never heard before! By using low quality headphones, you were missing out on quality in your music. Much like headphones, your voice recorder operates in the same fashion, which is why frequency response is so crucial.

## **DIGITAL VOICE RECORDERS**

As I stated before, most mini tape recorders were designed to cover typical human voice ranges, primarily for dictation purposes in an office or broadcast setting. After tape slowly died off, the digital voice recorder was born. Just like tape, all the digital voice recorders first produced were also made strictly for dictation, with extremely limited frequency ranges.

Quite a few cheaper digital voice recorders made today still cover these limited ranges. After all, they are made for dictation, so why cover frequencies that the average human speaking voice does not produce? This is where many experienced, even tech-savvy investigators, fail when it comes to purchasing equipment.

With the advent of portable music players, many manufactures have decided to make recorders with a much broader frequency range, so that the recorder itself can double as a portable music player. They not only produce higher frequencies for music purposes, but they can also record in these higher and lower frequencies as well, making them much better suited for EVP work.

A typical newer Olympus voice recorder will now cover an average range of 50-19,000HZ; much better than in the past with dictation type recorders!

Newer digital voice recorders cover more frequencies than older tape, which is clearly a bonus, and even more reason to stay clear of the older technology. But what other positive attributes do they have? The answer is many!

For starters, they are smaller and more compact, taking up less space than a pack of gum in your pocket, making them ideal for investigation. Next, they can be easily hooked up to a computer for file transfer. Some older digital models required the use of a now obsolete Serial Port, which made for extremely slow file data stream transfers. However, most recorders made today feature either a USB 2.0 dongle built right into the recorder, or come with a USB 2.0 cable for faster more reliable file transfers. Yet another reason to go digital, is the feature sets of these recorders. Now days most have an LCD back lit screen, making them easier to operate in dark environments, which also indicate the files sizes, current date and time, and the remaining time left on the recorder's internal memory. Couple these features with the fact that most digital recorders also have simple drag and drop interfaces in most versions of Microsoft Windows, are hot swappable, driverless plug and play, can also be used as a personal thumb drive, and you have a recipe for catching some exceptional evidence. Of course, while this all sounds good, there is still a significant drawback to most of these digital voice recorders on the market; file format and size!

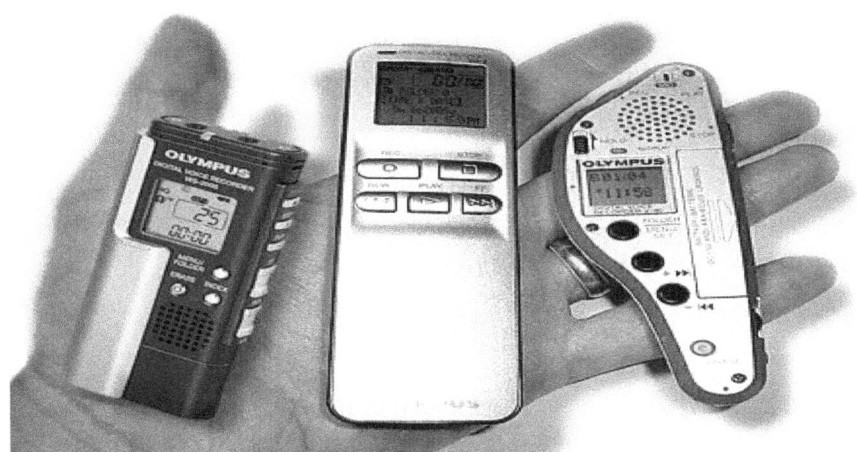

# **RECORDING FORMATS**

The two most common types of audio formats today are MP3 & WMA, or more technically knows as **MPEG Layer Three** and **Windows Media Audio**. Well, the audio files sound great on our little iPod's and other MP3 players, and wow, the files for these songs and audio files are so small that we can fit hundreds if not thousands of them on our players! How cool is that? Well, not so cool for paranormal investigation, where EVP and digital voice recorders are concerned.

MP3 or MPEG is an acronym for **Moving Picture Experts Group,** a working group of experts who were formed to set standards for audio and video compression and transmission, with attributes used for making video and audio smaller in size. Unfortunately, this results in a lossy format compared to the original. In order for us to fit all these videos and songs on our portable devices, they have to be shrunk in size from the original or compressed, otherwise, our favorite MP3 players and iPod's would need to be 10 times bigger than they are now. What happens to these files after they have been compressed, or made smaller? Well, what happens to something when we make it smaller? We have to remove pieces of it to make it fit! Imagine you are making a cake that calls for 4 cups of flour, but the bowl you are mixing it in only holds 3 cups, and it is the only bowl you have. Obviously, you would have to take some flour out of the recipe to make it work. The cake might come out less fluffy, but it will still be a cake in the end. Using the same approach to audio is no different, which is why many call MP3 or WMA formats lossy. If you were to listen to an original recording of your favorite song, and the same one in MP3, you would notice a substantial difference; not only in quality, but in file size as well.

Now, think about your digital voice recorder. It is pretty much the same thing as your iPod or other digital-music player; in that its main purpose is to store and play audio files in various formats, except it records as well.

Pay close attention to these formats your digital voice recorder records in! Look in your owner's manual, or at the file on your computer after you have transferred it. What are you seeing?

### If you are recording in either MP3 or WMA for EVP use, then you are recording in a "Lossy" format!

What you are recording into your voice recorder, and what is coming out, are two entirely different things! Your recorder is compressing all that audio you get from an investigation! It is happening to all of us who are recording in these popular lossy formats. What the recorder is picking up and what we are hearing are different! It is not hearsay, or some lame misconception, but the truth! So, what can be done to make sure that our recordings are not manipulated or compressed in order to save file space?

Unfortunately, it means spending more money, and purchasing a new recorder that records in a "lossless" format. The best format for paranormal recording is **.wav** format, or otherwise known as **WAV, WAVE, PCM or ADPCM,** which are all uncompressed formats, and retain all the original information in the recording. In fact, most veteran investigators in the field today will not even consider an EVP to be genuine unless it has been recorded in WAV format! Why?

### A MP3 or WMA file is 1/10th the size of a typical WAV file!!!!

Taking a sound, and compressing it down 10 times its normal size, is going to have adverse effects, and that is just simple common sense. If you do the math, you can see the results are alarming!

How much did you miss in your last EVP session? You will never know, and that is unacceptable! Why would we want to record in any other format as investigators? Sure, what you have is working for now, but how much are you missing in your recordings, and what price do you put on your self respect as an investigator?

Purchasing a recorder that records in WAV format is not that expensive. Recorders that utilize WAV format are normally around $99-$150, compared to ones that do not for around $30-$60.

Of course, there are a few drawbacks to using a recorder that records in WAV format. The first is obviously the cost of course, and the second is file size. Yes, as you read earlier, the size of a typical WAV file is going to be about 10 times bigger than the ones you are currently working with! Frustrating yes, but just think about how much more information is going to be contained in that audio file, and what new things are we going to hear? You can also count on that six-hour recording of you sleeping, being so large, that it will completely fill up your recorder. Obviously, the bigger the storage in your recorder, the better it is going to be for investigation purposes.

Most of these WAV style recorders only have around a 4GB storage capacity because of bit rate issues, but they all generally come with an extra built in memory card slot for adding more storage. For those of you who have laptops, you can also bring them with you on an investigation, and simply transfer the recorded files to make more room. While the files are much bigger on these recorders, and it may be a pain in the neck to deal with storage issues, I think these troubles are minor compared to the potential rewards.

Speaking of rewards, there is also another reason to start using these new recorders; frequency response! The typical MP3/WMA digital recorder you are using now is picking up frequencies typically around 50HZ-19,000HZ, which is perfectly acceptable for most. However, these newer recorders that utilize WAV format are capable of 20HZ-22,000HZ range, which means you are recording frequencies that you never have before; another reason to upgrade! I cannot stress enough how crucial it is to start recording in a lossless format such as WAV. I think the results that can be achieved will be worth the upgrade, and it will make any future evidence obtained that much more concrete in the paranormal community. Of course, you can still record in other formats, and it honestly will not hurt to record in MP3, if that is all you have. The American Association of Electronic Voice Phenomena (AAEVP) suggests recording in WMA if WAV is not available, or MP3 as a last resort. So, do not feel ashamed if you are using MP3 format. My intention here was not to criticize your equipment, but just to make you aware of certain limitations of that equipment.

# SELECTIVE RECORDING PHENOMENA

I have also come across an urban legend of sorts when it comes to frequency response and file format, which I like to call **SRP** or **Selective Recording Phenomena**. For years, I had often wondered why one voice recorder would pick up an EVP, and one sitting right next to it would not. This is actually quite simple to explain, and the answer is so simple, that it was easy to overlook. You see, if you have two different models of voice recorders sitting next to one another, the frequency coverage is going to be different between the two models. Recorder "A" might have a frequency response of 60-15,000HZ, while recorder "B" will have a range from 45-19,000HZ.

If you captured an EVP produced at 16,000HZ for example, obviously recorder "B" would have picked it up, and recorder "A" would have picked up nothing. I have even seen recorders of the same brand, and models do this as well. Besides frequency response, also throw in the fact that one recorder is recording in MP3 format, and the other in WMA, now you have even more variables causing confusion.

Another reason for SRP are the settings chosen in the recorders feature set. Most digital voice recorders have different microphone settings, and quality settings as well. An example of microphone settings would be "Conference" or "Dictation". The microphone is set to either a low (dictation) or high (conference) sensitivity; high hearing more, and low hearing less. Quality settings are examples such as: "XHQ" (Extra High Quality), "HQ" (High Quality), "LQ" (Low Quality), and "ULQ" (Ultra Low Quality). If you look at your voice recorder's owner's manual , you will see that the frequency range it records in depends on what quality it is set to.

The main reason this feature is provided, is so that users can choose how large their file sizes are; XHQ might take up the entire recorder's memory in two hours, where as ULQ will get you six hours on the memory. This is another reason why two recorders, which are identical, will often record different things at different times. It is not because of some mysterious force, or because a spirit decided to speak into one more than the other. It is simply a matter of knowing the settings on your equipment! If you have two different recorders, which have the same frequency response, file format and microphone sensitivity, you may still encounter SRP.

This could be caused by the chipsets in the two recorders being made by different manufacturers, the internal electronic parts being used by the spirit, or a number of different causes. My point here, is that SRP is not typically a phenomenon at all, and can easily be explained by simply getting to know your equipment. Make sure you know two things when you start recording with ANY digital voice recorder to help avoid Selective Recording Phenomena:

## ~ Know What Quality Setting Your Recording In ~
## ~ Know What Microphone Sensitivity Your Set At ~

A general rule of thumb is to keep your microphone set to its maximum sensitivity (Conference), and to select the highest quality recording size available. Do not miss those higher frequencies!

Many investigators do not even know their voice recorders have all these feature sets, or how they affect the evidence they collect.

Any investigator, regardless of experience, should know the specifications and limitations of their equipment, and Ignorance is not a valid excuse for missing potential evidence!

Every paranormal team I have come across in the past, has had a technical advisor. This is a team member who would take care of the technical aspects of the equipment, and instruct his or her team on its proper usage. While this is a fantastic idea, and I have had this prestigious title in the past, it is not a smart idea to rely on another person to know your equipment for you. It is your equipment. You purchased it, and you should learn how to use it, and properly operate it without needing to rely on someone else.

This is what owner's manuals are for, and if more investigators read them, and did the math, there would be less SRP, and uncertainty about evidence. I am sure there are genuine SRP's recorded, and I am not discrediting them completely, but proving they are genuine is extremely difficult. Even more so if we consider how many different explanations there are as to why they occur. Of course, some SRP could be legitimate, but such events are rare, in my opinion, and nearly impossible to validate.

# **FEATURES TO LOOK FOR**

I have purchased several different recorders over the years, and also made many suggestions to others on what to buy. Remember, you get what you pay for!

Most recorders of the same brand usually have the same features, with a few subtle differences. When it comes to different brands however, the features and specifications are quite different from one another. Finding one that will do everything you want it to do can be a tedious task, especially finding one that will record in WAV format. No matter what features you are looking for, and putting all of our individual tastes aside, I have come up with a list of essential features that you should look for when choosing a digital voice recorder for paranormal use. If you are going to take the leap and go digital, you should follow the following guidelines, and try not to cut any corners. Just try to follow these basic rules, and you should be well on your way to obtaining a reliable recorder:

**Never assume the recorder you choose has the features you want! Make sure the manufacturer states this important information on the package, owner's manual or web site!**

## ~ Frequency Response ~

This is perhaps the most important specification of any digital voice recorder. Try to find one that covers the broadest range of frequencies possible. Only a handful of manufactures will reveal the frequency coverage of any particular model, making it tough to find this information. If you cannot determine what its coverage is, try to find the information online by doing a search on the make and model you are interested in. If you still cannot find what you need to know, do not buy it! Buying a voice recorder without knowing this information, is like buying a pair of shoes without trying them on. Frequency response is everything!

## ~ File Format ~

As you read earlier, the best file formats to record in are WAV, PCM, or ADPCM (they are all the same). If you cannot afford this type or simply cannot find one, stick with one that records in WMA, as this format has less audio compression than MP3. If the model you are interested in does not state what format it records in, do not purchase or use it.

## ~ Computer Compatibility ~

Make sure the digital voice recorder has computer connectivity support such as USB or Serial support. This is a vital feature if you want to analyze your audio, or email audio files to your team members and clients. Most made today include this feature, but a handful still do not, so be careful what you choose to use. Moreover, try to find one that has a retractable USB dongle built in to the recorder itself, as this will eliminate the need to have a connection cable lying around. Do not be afraid to purchase a recorder that has the older Serial connection either. While this is a slower connection type, it is still useful. Just be sure that the computer you are hooking it up to has a Serial Port, as most new computers today no longer utilize this outdated technology.

## ~ Audio Inputs & Outputs ~

These features will allow you to hook up an external microphone to your recorder, and even allow the use of headphones that plug in directly. Some investigators will use a patch cable, and run it from the recorder's headphone output, straight into their laptop's microphone input, and by using recording software, they are able to monitor the frequencies they are recording live through the computer. I could go on and on about how many different ways you can utilize these features, so just make sure your recorder has these options. Most do, but some do not, so be careful.

## ~ Stereo Recording ~

More expensive models sold today, are recording in Stereo. This is done by the recorder's ability to record through a separate left and right channel, allowing the investigator to isolate these channels during review, so that they can listen to just one at a time. There are some recorders that are now using four channels, which allow for even more benefits. While recording in stereo is not a mandatory feature, I have included it here because the sound recorded through a stereo compatible recorder is night and day versus one that records in monotone. The ability to isolate just one channel during the review process is particularly handy as well. Most newer model's record in stereo now, and it is such a common feature today that most manufacturers do not even state they use it. Just double check anyway, as the prices between one that does and one that does not are small. If the recorder has two microphone ports built into the top, then it typically records in Stereo.

## ~ Backlit LCD Screen ~

This is just as it sounds; a screen that has been illuminated with a back light behind the screen. While this may seem like a luxury feature, it is more useful than most realize. It allows you to look at the screen, and adjust settings without having to turn on a flashlight, ruining your night vision. Most also produce enough light allowing it to be used for other purposes without blinding others, such as small area navigation.

Some manufactures even make the back light adjustable so it can be set to varying levels of brightness. You might have to shop around to find one that has a back-lit screen, but when you do find one, you will soon find that it also has many of the other features you are looking for that are listed here. Yes, it is true, that this back lighting can use up more battery life, but most only illuminate the screen when you are pressing a button, and quickly turn off 5-10 seconds after inactivity. While I highly recommend this feature, it is still not required. Like all other features you are looking for, be sure it states it has a back-lit screen before you purchase it!

## ~ Led Recording Light ~

I know this may sound insignificant at first, but this is actually a noteworthy feature. Do not ever assume that a spirit or ghost can see well at night, and do not assume that they will automatically know what that recorder your holding is used for. It could have some dark sinister purpose to them, and a **L.E.D.** (light-emitting diode emitting diode) will resolve these issues. Most recorders made today, will have a small, red or amber LED built in, which will blink or remain lit, confirming that the unit is recording. This is not only positive because it gives the investigator a visual confirmation that the unit is functioning properly, but it also gives the spirit or ghost something to focus its energy on. If you were a ghost, and an investigator said to you: "See this little red light, come speak into it and I will be able to hear you." would you go to the light and try to communicate?

Plus, if it is placed in a location that is extremely dark without an LED light, how would a potential spirit even know it was there or how to find it? Just by having this little feature, you are increasing your chances of getting evidence dramatically! Most manufactures make their recorders with this feature, but like usual, some do not. Double check to make sure it says, "LED Record Light" or "LED Recording Indicator".

## ~ Driverless Operation or Plug & Play ~

All too often, I see investigators buy a digital voice recorder which cannot be used on a computer without installing software that allows the device to work. I try my best to avoid such devices, and for a worthy reason; you should never have to rely on software for your recorder to operate. I dislike having to install any more software on my computer than necessary, because all it does is complicate things. I have been with many teams in the past, and I cannot count how many times I have had to download software because a team member's recorder needed it in order to transfer files to my computer. Then, the recorder used some strange file format (VOC for example) that the software needed, just so my computer could read it.

**What if you are on an investigation, and you need to transfer files to your laptop in order to free up memory, but you forgot your software? What if you upgrade your version of Windows on your computer, but the software for your recorder does not support the upgrade? What if the manufacturer of your recorder goes out of business, and you can no longer obtain support for the software?**

Seriously, Plug & Play means just that. You can plug in the recorder to your computer, and play the files-simple and without the need to install any software. There are many companies out there, who require software for their recorders, and the most popular ones are Sony and RCA. In fact, most everything Sony makes requires some type of proprietary software or hardware to work properly. This is just a scheme to get more money from consumers, in my opinion. I like Sony products, but as far as voice recorders go, I stay clear of them. Of course, there are models that Sony makes which are Plug & Play, but I have not seen too many of them. Now, there are some recorders out there with excellent features, which make going proprietary worth the sacrifice. Some record in WAV format for example, but they are few and far between.

## ~ Accepts Standard Batteries ~

I have seen many decent voice recorders, whose only faults were that they utilized a specialized rechargeable battery pack. Now, recharging your voice recorder's battery to save money might seem like a good idea, but only if the battery is easily replaced at a moment's notice. Over time, a rechargeable battery will eventually have to be discarded, and replaced because it will no longer maintain an adequate charge. How much is this special battery pack going to cost you, and where do you find it in a pinch? Is saving a few bucks worth taking the risk of having to leave your recorder in your pocket during an investigation? What if there is no power on the property to recharge the battery, or it failed, and is no longer usable? I have seen this situation before, and it is extremely frustrating.

While much of your equipment as an investigator will mainly rely on rechargeable batteries, I personally do not think that your recorder should if you can avoid it. Make sure the recorder you purchase will accept standard **Alkaline**, **NIMH**, or **Li-ion** batteries in the standard sizes such as A, AA, or AAA. It is acceptable to use rechargeable batteries in the standard sizes, because the recorder will not know the difference between an alkaline and a rechargeable, and if your rechargeable battery does fail, you can just simply replace it with an alkaline battery and keep recording. In general, I would stay clear of recorders that utilize <u>special</u> batteries, regardless of features.

If you are going to use a recorder that has a proprietary battery pack, make sure you purchase several spares of the same type, just in case you have a battery failure. Battery failures happen quite often during a paranormal investigation, and all investigators should be prepared for them. There is nothing worse than having usable equipment sitting in your equipment case because you cannot get a fresh battery for it.

## ~ Brand Recognition ~

How many times have you heard this: "If the item you're thinking about purchasing is made by a popular well known company, chances are, you're getting a quality product"? While this is true, for the most part, there are still some well known companies out there that still make an inferior product, so it is all relative.

RCA is a company with a long history of audio experience, but the digital voice recorders they make have terrible features. Some require software to run, and company support is pretty much worthless. The same also goes for some generic companies as well.

I purchased a digital voice recorder years ago from an overseas supplier in China through EBay. The recorder was great looking, had all the features I wanted, and was about half the price of one comparable here in the states. Well, it did not take more than five minutes after I received it to figure out it was garbage. I think a general rule of thumb here, is to go with companies that have been making the product for a long time. For example, Olympus has been making voice recorders for over 30 years, and Sanyo has been making them for quite some time as well, so purchasing from either one of them is a no brainer. There are also online merchants who sell brands like Zoom and Tascam, and while these recorders are a good value for the money, they can be geared towards a more professional type of audio recording, and some of the built in features can actually hinder you progress.

Look for reviews on the product before you buy it. One way to do this, is to search the exact product you are looking for through Amazon.com. They usually have many reviews on the product, and I have even left a few myself. Another place for a review is cnet.com. When I look for a voice recorder, I normally look to one company first, and that is Olympus. They have a long positive history in the paranormal community, and I suggest you start your search with them. However, if you are going to purchase one of their models online, do so through sites like Amazon, EBay, Buy.com, Overstock.com, etc. Buying straight from the manufacturer will usually cost you more money.

## ~ Expandable Memory ~

Simply put, this is additional memory storage for your recorder. Most recorders that utilize MP3 or WMA formats are not made with additional storage because of how small the files are, and there is simply no need for additional storage (unless it plays music also).

However, if you are recording in larger formats such as WAV, look for a recorder with additional storage options. Internal built in memory can be filled up in just a few hours, even on a 4GB recorder when recording in WAV. By having the ability to plug in additional memory cards, you can eliminate the need to transfer files when your memory is full. Most recorders that utilize WAV format have expandable memory capability, but there are some available on the market that do not, so pay attention.

## ~ Recommendations ~

Contrary to the popular belief, one does not have to spend a small fortune for a voice recorder. You can find decent models that will have all the features mentioned here, for under $200. As I mentioned before, a $30 recorder that records in MP3 or WMA can be used, but because I do not agree with recording in these lossy formats, I cannot give these types of recorders my personal recommendation for paranormal use. Here are just a few examples of what I consider to be decent voice recorders, and they all have the features mentioned in this chapter:

Olympus WS-700M
Olympus WS-710M
Olympus DM-620
Olympus DM-520
Olympus LS-7

Sony ICD-UX512
Sony ICD-SX712D
Sony ICD-UX513F

Tascam DR-08
Tascam PR-10
Tascam VR-10

Zoom H1 Ultra
Zoom H2 Ultra

Teac VR-10

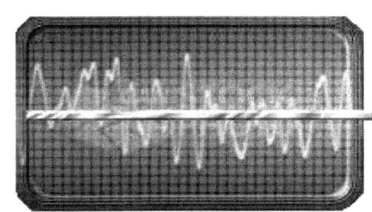

# ~ CHAPTER FOUR ~
## RECORDING TECHNIQUES & GUIDELINES

Just like everything else in the paranormal, when it comes to technique, it is all mostly a matter of personal taste. However, there are still things you should know that will produce better results, and make your evidence gathering more productive. The main focus of your EVP work will be picking up residual or intelligent audio recordings, and the best way to accomplish this will be through direct contact with the environment through the use of your own voice, coupled with equipment that can record it. You might think that simply sneaking around and asking questions would provide the best results. While this is primarily true, there are other techniques that should be used to encourage the past to replay, or to make an intelligent spirit speak to you. Words truly cannot describe the thrill of recording an EVP, or especially an AVP for the first time. Knowing that you captured something that could possibly be from beyond, and that may have been directly responding to you at the time, is addicting to say the least.

EVP's are like really good potato chips; nobody can eat just one!

I will just list some basic rules for questioning, and then I will go into some more advanced techniques, and of course include things not to do. Before I do that, first let us start by going through the preparations that are needed before you're ready to walk through that haunted building, and wake up all those sleeping spirits! A little preparation will go a long way!

# PRELIMINARY'S

Before you or any of your team even leaves the house, no matter what location you are investigating, you should research the property and perform a brief history on the land as well.

You need to know everything, no matter how insignificant the detail. Was there a fire? Was there a death? Who died, and when?

Get as much information on the location as you can, as this will make you a better investigator. At least half of paranormal investigation is performed in the library or at the historical archives.

It is also spent interviewing those directly affected by the phenomena, and their friends or neighbors. The more information you walk into a location with, the better your chances for evidence and proper review later. Imagine a woman named Mary dies in her home, from taking a terrible fall down the stairs. While investigating, you hear what sounds like rumbling coming from the staircase.

Obviously, these sounds would make much more sense after knowing the history of the location. When did the family live there? Where in the residence did Mary sleep, and what was here favorite room? Did Mary have a favorite color? My point here is simple:
**Research! Research! Research!**


Proper preparation does not include just research alone, it also includes your equipment. Do you have enough batteries and flashlights? Do you have headphones? Do you have enough warm clothing? It is better having too much equipment with you than not enough. Wear dark clothing, and the reason for this is a simple one; you do not want anything following you home! Spirits can be attracted to bright colors, and can become attached to them, so wear dark colors! Furthermore, make sure the clothes you wear are quiet. I cannot tell you how many times I have investigated with those who chose to wear nylon type fabrics, resulting in "whooshing" sounds from moving around. Remember, the microphones on digital voice recorders are extremely sensitive, and even the smallest sounds are amplified. There is nothing worse than listening to your recordings the next day only to hear the sounds of nylon Parachute Pants, or a Gortex Jacket!

Another thing to remember; bring more than one investigator along with you! Some of the old buildings I have been in were dangerous, and it would have been foolish to investigate alone. If a significant event happens like a manifestation, or a class 1 AVP is heard, it is always gratifying to have someone there to corroborate your evidence. If you are going to a remote location where there is no cell phone coverage, or help to be found, make sure you tell someone where you are going in case of an emergency. If investigating a large location, and you plan on splitting up with your team to cover more ground, two way radios are a wise investment, and can be purchased for around $30. Make sure to turn off your cell phone, as EMF interference can be recorded by your voice recorder or other equipment. Even if you are not using it, a cell phone will periodically attempt to connect or "Ping" to your service provider, and this can produce all kinds of interference, even more so if you have a data plan.

Make sure you have plenty of liquids to drink, and if you are packing food, make sure the food you bring is quiet. Having to listen over a loud potafo chip bag or candy bar wrapper is extremely annoying, and can mask not only potential evidence on your recorder, but audible evidence to your ears!

I know it may be expensive, but having an additional voice recorder is also a smart idea, or at least have someone from your team bring a spare. You never know what events might occur, which could damage your equipment. Getting into some of these popular haunted locations can be expensive, and the last thing you need is to waste time and money. So, if you can, bring backup! In addition, make note of the weather conditions at your location, as there is currently much research being done on the links between atmospheric conditions and paranormal activity.

Things like electrical storms, earthquakes, moon phase, and barometric pressure have been shown to affect evidence. Some investigators will bring weather stations along with them to monitor changes in the environment, and I encourage this practice.

# THE INVESTIGATION

Who, What, Where, When, Why and How; these are the questions you need to ask when doing any paranormal research.

Remember, you are on an investigation, just like a detective at the scene of a crime, or a journalist getting a story. It is crucial that you ask these essential questions, and stick to the following rules:

## ~ Scheduling ~

Entities can speak at any time of day or night. If you are going to be investigating the same location multiple times, it may be in your benefit to start at a regular time. By doing this, the entities can learn when there will be an opportunity for communication. This can also boost the trust factor between you and any potential spirits. Of course, going back at different times can yield different evidence as well, and there is no manual that states spirit activity only occurs at night. So, if multiple investigations are warranted, you should pay close attention to when and what time you decide to return. The information you obtained when performing your research could very well dictate this for you.

## ~ Request Protection For You & Your Team ~

While I have personally never been attacked by the spirits I have investigated, I have been touched. Being touched can leave you with the feeling that you are vulnerable, and some investigators do not process this very well. Having a finger being poked into your back, or your shoulder being brushed against will usually turn most investigators in a wad of cookie dough. You never know what events are going to transpire during an investigation, which is why I suggest being protected. This is the very first thing you should do before walking into any investigation, and all those investigating should be involved.

The simplest way to protect you and your team, is to say a little prayer together before entering any investigative location. Regardless of your religious beliefs, it is a scientifically proven fact that prayer works, and it can be a powerful ally. No need for candles and a Bible, just a simple team prayer to give thanks for the opportunity, and ask for protection will suffice. Another way to protect yourself, is to make sure you and your team represent yourselves honestly and ethically, while respecting the spirits you are investigating. Stumbling around screaming and leaving your trash behind helps nobody, and it's no secret the most polite and respectful investigators are the ones who achieve the best results.

I would also like to point out, the power of your own voice. From my experience, most spirits weather they are Malevolent or Benevolent in nature, are subject to earth bound laws. One of these laws states that if you tell them to leave you alone, they must obey, and most do. Take a stand, with a commanding voice, and tell them to leave you and your team alone, and that they are no longer welcome in your presence. Most cases that involve a residential haunting are resolved in this manner by the residents and home owners themselves, without the need for any type of cleansing. When done with your investigation, make sure you tell any spirits they are not welcome to leave with you, and that they must remain there...you don't want any hitchhikers following you home!

Also, never investigate your own home unless you are prepared to accept the evidence you may obtain. I remember one investigation I did several years ago, in which a young married couple wanted an investigation of the small apartment they lived in. After a thorough investigation, much evidence was obtained in the form of EVP. After hearing these recordings, some of which directly mentioned them, they were terrified to continue living there, and moved out months later. Activity did not increase in the apartment, but just the fact they we had proof of other worldly spirits dwelling there made them feel uncomfortable enough to move. Of course, spirit activity could have increased after opening up the door of communication, which is another reason to be careful when investigating your own residence. So, if you are going to investigate your own residence, make sure you are emotionally prepared to accept the truth, and live with the potential consequences.

## ~ Background Source/Transform ~

Research has shown that in **Transform EVP or ITC,** the entities use sounds in the environment to help form words. Most recording situations have some background sounds, but it may be necessary to add noise with something like a fan or running water. Some people use foreign language radio, crowd babble, audio tapes and Franks Boxes, but the AAEVP discourages the use of radio static or live voice of any form to avoid false positives. I have, however, heard live voice produce undeniable evidence, so it really comes down to personal taste. The transform method can produce very positive results, so regardless of what others may tell you, I suggest keeping your mind open to the technique.

## ~ Get To Know Your Recorder ~

If you are using a new voice recorder for the first time, or using another team member's recorder, make sure you familiarize yourself with all of its features and functions. Spend some time getting used to where all of the buttons are, and what they do, so you can operate them in dark conditions. I can't tell you how frustrating it can be having a team member clicking on their flashlight in order to find a certain button on their recorder, ruining everybody's night vision. This not only makes you a more efficient investigator, but it also prevents others from being disturbed.

Speaking of disturbing your fellow investigators, you will also need to turn off your recorder's beep confirmation function, if it has this ability. Many recorders, like the ones I use, have the ability to produce a beeping sound when any button is pressed. While this may sound cool, it can be annoying to other investigators. Having to hear a million beeps when playing with the features on your voice recorder is not only frustrating to other investigators, but it can also mask potential evidence in the immediate area. Not all recorders will have the option to turn this feature off, so if this is the case, try to limit the amount of button presses you perform, or try leaving the room until you get your recorder set the way you like it.

## ~ Keep Your Recorder Away From Your Body ~

Remember, you are recording what is around you, not the sound of you breathing, or the sound your jacket makes. If you are using an external microphone, you can carry the recorder on you, but keep the microphone a safe distance away from you. A comfortable reach in any direction is usually sufficient. Some like to hang them around their necks, Velcro them to clothing in order to free up an extra hand, but I discourage this practice. To keep recordings genuine, you need to try and eliminate false positives, and one of the best ways to do this is to keep the recorder isolated from your body movements. If you still decide to attach your recorder to your body, find a location that is quiet, like on your upper arm or other location that does not rub on clothing, by using an armband designed for an iPod.

## ~ Keep Your Fingers Away From The Microphone ~

When holding your recorder, pay close attention to where your fingers are, and keep them away from the built-in microphone ports. Your recorder is extremely sensitive, and your fingers moving around the outside of the recorder, and over the microphone ports will drown out possible evidence.

## ~ State The Date, Time, & All Investigators Present

It is essential to make sure you state the date and time on your recordings every time you record a session. In addition, make sure you state where you are in the building, which investigators are present with you, and any other information you feel may be useful. This eliminates the confusion later that might arise from hearing a fellow investigator make a strange noise, and even help you pinpoint which area an EVP was recorded in. Most new digital voice recorders automatically attach a date and time stamp on all recordings, but it is still an excellent idea to state it yourself. If you are using multiple recorders make sure you state that information by mentioning the make and model of your recorders also.

## ~ Don't Whisper ~

If you are going to speak, do so in a normal calm voice, and never whisper. EVP in the "B" Class, which are the most common, typically sound like a whisper, so it is extremely important to make sure that you, and fellow investigators, follow this rule. Even the most seasoned investigator will find that it is instinct to want to whisper when recording is taking place, and it is hard to combat this at times. If you whisper, or you hear another investigator whisper, just make sure you state it on the recording to save aggravation later.

## ~ Record All Investigators Voices ~

While you think you may know the sound of all your investigator's voices, they may sound different on your recordings. To avoid your fellow teammates sounding like a potential spirit, record each of their voices on the recorder you are going to use, by having each of them state their names in a normal speaking voice, and then again whispering. If you come across a voice or whisper later that you think might be one of your teammates, then you will have a baseline recording to compare. It is an excellent idea to do this for each recorder, and have each team member keep these recordings on file for later use.

## ~ State The Obvious ~

Often, you will hear sounds in your environment that will be picked up on your recorder. Things like airplanes, traffic passing by, dogs barking, a heater kicking on, an investigator's stomach growling; these can all be very frustrating, so make sure you state what the sound is on your recording, if you hear one. If you hear your name whispered in your ear, a knock, or your K2 or other EMF meter goes crazy, you should note that on the recording for later reference also. The more information you give about what is going on in the environment, the better off you are in the long run. Moreover, just before taking a picture, make sure you say "Flash" so the sound of your camera is not mistaken for evidence. This also gives your fellow investigators a chance to look away before being blinded.

## ~ State Who You Are & Why You Are There ~

Remember, you are a stranger to a spirit or ghost, and if you want them to open up to you, it might help you if they know who you are, why you are there or what your intentions are. Treat them like you would any person you are meeting for the first time by being polite. Inform them that you are only there to speak to them. It is crucial that they know you are not going to hurt them, and that you are there to help. This will often open up the door of communication better than any other method, and the potential rewards can be great!

## ~ Be Polite ~

Just because a person has passed on, does not mean they do not deserve respect. If you were a spirit, would you respond to some stranger being rude and demanding? Remember to say please and thank you, and show respect to those on the other side, as your odds on getting evidence increase 100 fold! Also, you do not want any potential spirit getting aggravated, and taking that frustration out on the client after you and your team leave. You attract more Bears with honey than vinegar!

## ~ Ask Simple Questions ~

It takes a great deal of energy for spirits to talk to you and answer your questions, so it is suggested that your questions be simple to answer. If you ask them to recite Gone with the Wind, chances are you are not going to get a response. Yes, or no questions tend to be the best for starters, and then ask more personal questions later after the potential spirit has warmed up to you. If you get a response to your question or specific request in real time, make sure to ask the spirit to do it one more time, as this will help confirm that you have captured legitimate evidence. Very rarely will it ever happen twice, but if it does, you can tell all those skeptics to go you know where.

## ~ Try Not To Provoke ~

**Provoking,** is the act of stimulating a response through the use of a commanding voice, while getting personal, direct or offensive.

While using this technique can sometimes yield evidence, it is only recommended as a last resort. Remember, this technique can also have negative effects as well, not only to you and your fellow investigators, but to your client after you leave! Normally, negative energy will have the same effect on you as it does any potential spirit. Be extremely careful if you decide to use provoking methods, as it has been documented, that investigators can be harmed when using these techniques. You also do not want any of your expensive equipment being damaged by a frustrated spirit. Having a $500 infrared digital camcorder and tripod fall to the ground is great evidence, but it's also an expensive lesson as well.

## ~ Give Time For A Response ~

Give 5-10 seconds after each question to make sure you give enough time for a response. Rifling through questions right after one another will get you nowhere fast. Spirits need time to get the energy required to respond to you, so give it to them.

## ~ Do Not Talk Over One Another & Stay Put ~

When someone on your team is doing an EVP session, try not to interrupt or talk over them. Do not be that annoying person on the team who talks continuously, or is constantly moving around the room making noise. It is unfortunate when good evidence has to be discarded because you, or a fellow team member, made noise talking or making an old floor creak. Move from location to location, but do it quietly, and with respect to your fellow investigators.

## ~ Describe Your Equipment ~

The spirits you are investigating need to know what the equipment you are using does. Make sure you state you are holding a recording device, and that you are able to hear them if they speak into it. If your recorder has a LED light that lights up during recording, tell them to talk to the little red light, or orange, whatever the case may be. Also, make sure that any other equipment your holding at the time is explained as well. The twinkling lights of a K2, or the beeping of a Cell Sensor can scare away a potential spirit if they do not know what those devices are used for. Never just assume that any potential spirit knows what you are doing, and why. Be courteous and reap the rewards!

## Techniques

In addition to the guidelines mentioned, here are some techniques for recording, which yield really good results:

## ~ Recording In Wind ~

As paranormal investigators, often times we are not limited to just investigating indoors. In fact, from my personal experiences, I have found that at least 40% of the locations I have investigated have taken place outdoors. Even when the main focus was inside a building or residence, investigating the grounds outside was also a priority. When it comes to audio recording outdoors, there is one factor that can be the difference between a successful recording session, and no session at all; wind.

Windy conditions are next to impossible to record in. Not only is it difficult to ascertain sounds in the immediate environment, but the buffering sounds that a voice recorder will pick up, make listening to possible evidence later extremely problematic. I have seen some very interesting gadgets in my travels, which were designed to combat windy conditions, but most of them failed, or made the recordings too muffled.

Unfortunately, there is no simple solution to completely eliminate the buffering caused by wind, but if postponing your investigation is not an option, there are a few techniques you can use, which can limit the effects of Mother Nature. One method I like to use is to take note of the wind's direction, and simply turn my back to it, holding my recorder under a hat or baseball cap. You can also try using a windscreen. A windscreen is simply a piece of cloth or foam, which covers over the recorder's microphone ports. There are a few manufacturers, who make wind screens for some of their products, but they are very limited in availability, and only work with the more expensive professional recorders.

If you cannot obtain a wind screen for your particular recorder, you can just simply make one for next to nothing. Foam padding can be found at most home improvement outlets, and most craft stores as well. Even your local hardware store can provide protective foam. When making your own wind screen, be sure to put some thin fabric behind the foam, like material from an old cotton shirt, as this will catch any wind that may pass through the foam.

Wrapping the recorder in a pair of thin socks can also yield pretty good results. One thing to keep in mind is the recorder's microphone sensitivity setting. Try setting your recorder to "Dictation" instead of "Conference" when in windy conditions. As mentioned in an earlier chapter, "Dictation" mode is less sensitive, and may help reduce unwanted wind noise. Just make sure to change the setting back to "Conference" when you are finished, or heading back indoors.

## ~ Group Sessions ~

Perhaps the most popular type of EVP gathering, and the one that yields the most evidence, is the group recording method. This is where all investigators record together in the same room or area, and each team member has a recorder. Since all spirits need to use energy they obtain from the environment in order to communicate, having energy from additional investigators together really helps to obtain evidence.

One of the most important things to remember when doing a group session, is to make sure you give each investigator a chance to ask questions. You might find that the spirit will respond to one investigator more than the other. Sometimes a male will get more responses from a female spirit, and vice versa. In addition, since most investigators use different types of equipment, some recorders might pick up more evidence than others, which is why it is important to make sure that several different brands of recorders are used. Make sure to have at least one person in your group listening to the evidence in real time by wearing headphones. Most recorders made today will allow you to plug in a set of headphones, which will allow you to hear what you are recording in real time.

## ~ Single Person Session ~

Many times, I have investigated places that were known to have a great deal of activity, only to go home with nothing. A main contributor to this, was having too many people in one location at a time. Having six or eight investigators in a single room can intimidate any spirit. So, to avoid this, try to make sure there are only 2-4 of you in any room at a time. If you are going to attempt to record alone, make sure a static (stationary) camera is recording in the room with you just in case you have an encounter.

## ~ Burst EVP Session ~

This is a method that allows for immediate review of short term recording sessions. Simply put, you record a session of no more than five to ten minutes, and immediately stop recording to review any possible evidence you may have captured right at the scene. This is a very successful method of analysis, because any evidence collected allows the possibility of two-way conversation, and direct interaction with the spirit in real time. Remember, not all recorders will capture evidence due to frequency response and sensitivity settings, so it is important to make sure that multiple members of your team be involved in burst recording. Various methods can be used to review evidence on scene, such as downloading your recording onto a laptop to review evidence, or by simply plugging in a set of headphones into your recorder and playing the file.

## ~ VOR ~

Another method is to use the **VOR** feature on your recorder, which enables **voice operated recording**. When using this feature, your recorder will not start recording until a sound is picked up by the recorder's microphone. If you synchronize two recorders, and use the VOR feature on both, and start recording them both at the same time, you can stop the recording after a specific amount of time and compare the two in recording time. If one recorder has recorded more than the other, you can determine which recorder picked up something, and which one did not, and immediately review the evidence on that specific recorder.

There is of course a downfall to using VOR, and that is a delay in recording time. Most recorders when using the VOR feature, will have a one or two second delay from the time they pick up a sound until the time they actually record it, which of course is not acceptable. Considering that most EVP is very subtle, and will not trigger the VOR feature anyway, I really do not suggest using this method of recording as your primary technique for EVP gathering. I suggest only trying this as a supplement to direct recording.

## ~ Stand Alone Method ~

We do not always have to be present to record an EVP. In fact, many investigators achieve excellent results leaving the recorder in a specific location, and coming back several hours later to review possible evidence. This is called stand alone recording.  Face it, some of us can be quite intimidating to a potential spirit, and this is where stand alone recording comes in handy. Not only can this method persuade a potential spirit to open up, it can also make our job as investigators easier when we have other rooms to investigate.

If you are going to use this method of recording, be sure to leave the recorder in a location you think has the most activity, and the least amount of noise as well. If there is noise such as traffic or a heater kicking on, make sure to state it at the beginning of your recording, as well as which room you are in. Another essential thing to remember, is to make sure you tell any potential spirit in the room you are leaving a recording device behind, and that you would like them to speak into it. Make sure the batteries are fresh, especially if you have been using the recorder for hours prior, as spirit activity has a tendency to drain batteries. It is also advisable to have another recorder in the room along with your own for credibility and debunking purposes. The most important thing to remember, is to have a video camera recording the area where the recorder is sitting. Often, a recorder will be sitting in a slightly different position than it was left in, and failing to document this movement can be frustrating, to say the least. Be sure document your recorder's exact position by placing a small piece of paper underneath it and outlining one edge of it with a faint pencil mark. If you want to encourage movement of your recorder, you can always place a trigger object right next to it in hopes that the potential spirit will be tempted to move it. Be sure to inform other investigators that you have set up a recorder, so they do not inadvertently walk into the area creating confusion on the recording.

## ~ Transform Method/ITC ~

**Transform EVP:** Traditionally, EVP formation has involved the transformation of available audio-frequency energy into voice, which is thought to occur in the electronic equipment. The resulting signal is seen as a simulation of human voice, which may very closely mimic the physical voice of the person thought to be speaking. This includes accent, age, sex and attitude. Transform EVP was traditionally accomplished by using radio static (white noise) as background sound. Current practices involve the use of unmodulated noise, such as supplied by a fan, but most EVP are recorded today using a digital voice recorder. Many investigators still use this method, even though they use such equipment.

This technique can be seen in the motion picture White Noise. ITC techniques have evolved in recent years, and it is possible to use background noise without radio interference. The best way to produce a background noise that is more reliable than the ghost box method, is using a CD (or MP3 files) containing random **phonemes** (discussed later) previously recorded. For example: "Cau Ro Val Whe Bo Na Fer Mis Sum Ma Es, etc."

It is important that the phonemes do not mean anything when put together, so that investigators know that the messages were not previously recorded on the CD. There must be at least a hundred and fifty different phonemes recorded and repeated for at least twenty minutes of recording in order to have good material to be shaped into sentences by spirits. When investigators listen to the CD without spiritual communication, this is what will be heard: "caurovalwhebonafermissummaes...." and once the communication starts, these phonemes are transformed by spirits into superimposed sentences, which may become: "Hel lo, I am he re an d I ca n hea ryou" or whatever sentence they want to make.

If the copy of the same CD (the original one without the spiritual message) is used for all communication, and yet, every message has a different content, it means that there is no way that the sentences were previously recorded. Once the messages are recorded, it may be a good idea to ask a few people that are unrelated to the investigation to hear the recordings and judge what they think the sentences mean. If most of them understand the same thing without having to listen twice, this indicates a good possibility that the messages are real.

## ~ Opportunistic Method/The Ghost Box ~

In the last several years, another method of EVP gathering has gained popularity in the paranormal community. It enables potential spirits to speak directly to you through the use of white noise with no recording device needed; it is called a Ghost Box, or more commonly known as a **Frank's Box**, and is another form of ITC.

Created in 2002 by EVP enthusiast **Frank Sumption** for supposed real-time communication with the dead, Sumption claims he received his design instructions from the spirit world. The device is a combination white noise generator, and AM radio receiver modified to sweep back and forth through the AM radio band without stopping on any single station. This linear sweeping of the band allows the user to hear not only the static or white noise, but also all radio signals in the area which are passed by so quickly, only small snippets of sounds and words are heard, giving any potential spirit a good medium for direct contact. Critics of the device say its effect is subjective and incapable of being replicated, and since it relies on radio noise, any meaningful response a user gets is purely coincidental, or simply the result of audible matrixing, which is where the term "**Opportunistic Recording**" comes from. However, any paranormal investigator who has used one for any great length of time will quickly disagree.

It should be noted that these types of devices should only be used as a basis to note possible activity, used in conjunction with a separate voice recorder, and the evidence gathered from them should only be taken seriously if corroborated by other recording equipment. While the original models of the Frank's Box were extremely large and not very portable, many inventors and electronic enthusiasts have developed ways to make their own for very little cost, while being extremely portable. I have personally made and used these smaller versions of the Frank's Box, and while they are not as functional as the original, they can still produce decent evidence.

If you would like to make your own Frank's Box, all you need to do is search YouTube on the term "Shack Hack" or "Frank's Box Hack", and you will find many videos posted that will instruct you on how to make your own for as little as $30. You can also find them readily available on EBay for around $50. I have personally used these devices, and they are well worth the time. If you own one, here are some field-tested guidelines for using one below. If you do not own a Ghost Box, I still suggest reading the guidelines anyway. You never know who you might run into, that could require your expert advice on how to use one.

# * Get To Know Your Radio *

The first thing you should do before taking your new Ghost Box into the field, is familiarize yourself with its basic features. I suggest that you read the owner's manual that came with your radio, and get used to where the buttons are, so that you may operate the unit easily in dark environments. Practice using one-handed operation so that you can still carry other equipment if needed. Always use fresh batteries, and always carry a few extra sets with you. Like with any equipment you use for paranormal investigating, always be prepared to replace the batteries.

Test your new radio's functions, and know its basic design. Operate all the buttons and familiarize yourself with how much pressure they require to activate, where they are located, and what they do.

Remember, the majority of investigations take place at night under low lighting, so make sure you know where the buttons are without the need to use a flashlight. Get used to how sensitive the reception is by moving around the room with the radio operating.

The better you familiarize yourself with the features and quirks, the more proficient you will be at using it during an actual investigation. This same process is also recommended for your digital voice recorder and other equipment as well.

# * Basic Scanning Operation *

The Ghost Box has been modified to do a linear sweep of either the AM or FM bands without stopping using the station scan or seek feature. Start this by simply choosing a band with the band select buttons, and holding down either scan button (up or down) for a few seconds. You will notice that not only does the unit keep scanning even though it has picked up a clear signal, but you can also hear the stations as it passes by them. This is the heart of the modification, and it is what gives the radio its unique Ghost Box functionality.

You will notice that the FM band has more bits of music than the AM band does. Obviously, this is because the FM band is more widely used. The AM band, however, does not have as much music, and has more talk related programming, and static. It is for this reason, that the AM band is more widely used for paranormal purposes. With all the speech and static, it gives a potential spirit more of a platform to speak to you, and I highly suggest using this band to start out. Now, I am not saying that the FM band is useless, and I have had just as much success on the FM band as I have the AM band, so experiment with both during an investigation. Things like location, the earth's rotation, atmospheric conditions, battery power, interference, and how the radio is held in relation to the antenna, will all impact available reception, and what type of evidence you obtain. Furthermore, understand that the AM band requires an entirely different frequency modulation, so it is much more sensitive to environmental conditions. I highly suggest switching to a different band on occasion, just to keep your potential evidence genuine.

Another thing to be aware of is the direction of the scan, and how it affects your evidence. This is something even seasoned investigators overlook when using a Ghost Box Radio, and unless you are aware of it, you can miss potential evidence. This may be a little hard to understand, so I will try to be as remedial as possible. For this example, we will use the FM band. So, you are in FM mode, and scanning the band while looking at the screen. You notice that you are currently scanning in a forward direction; you are scanning from the lowest frequency to the highest. Now, let us imagine when you hit 97.3FM on the scan you hear the word "Hello", and just after at 101.5FM you hear "Goodbye". First you hear "Hello" and next you hear "Goodbye" in that order. Well, now turn back the clock, and imagine you were scanning backwards this time; from high to low frequency. In this case, you would have heard the word "Goodbye" first and then the word "Hello" last. This is an extremely important point to understand, because depending on your question at the time, one word could have made sense and answered your question, while the other made no sense at all.

If you were scanning in a different direction, the opposite would be true. So, how do we know which direction to scan in? Simple, use both! If you are having trouble getting a response in one direction, try using the other and switch back and forth. One thing to be on the lookout for, is the type of voice you are hearing. If you are hearing the same type of voice on different frequencies, and in different directions, this is a very good sign that you may be directly communicating with the other side! By changing to different bands, you can help determine the validity of your potential evidence. So, when scanning, remember to switch bands on occasion, and switch scan direction also!

## * Scanning During An Investigation *

Like any other piece of equipment in your arsenal, you need to be able to spot which conditions they work best in. Sometimes, depending on your location, you will see that like any radio, your ability to bring in distant signals could be limited. However, just because you cannot bring in any stations, does not automatically mean that your radio will not work. While you should have at least static or white noise for it to function properly, you do not always need to have speech, and many investigators favor this. Below is a list of things to keep in mind during scanning:

- Remember, spirits do not typically stay in one location in a residence, they move around. If you think you were getting evidence, and suddenly it stopped, try moving to another location in the building. If you find you are getting responses again, make sure you log that information down for future reference. This could very well give you a pattern or blueprint of the spirits moving habits, and your new Ghost Box, is an excellent tool for doing just that! Your EMF meters might not always give you this information, but your Ghost Box will, if the spirit is willing to communicate with you.

✪ When doing your preliminary check of the location, be sure to log down areas of high <u>explained</u> or natural EMF readings, and keep your Ghost Box away from these locations, as the interference could have adverse effects on your radio giving you false positives.


✪ When asking questions, make sure you speak in a pleasant non threatening voice, and ask short easy to answer questions, such as: "Are you here?", "What is your name?", "How Old Are You?" etc. The easier the question is to answer, the better your odds on getting a response. Spirits take a great deal of energy to speak to us, so making them give you a long drawn-out answer to a complicated question is not going to yield you very many results. In addition, remember to say thank you if you think you have had a response, and be polite! Remember, you catch more Bears with honey than with vinegar!

✪ Wait at least 10 seconds before asking another question. Remember to give the spirit time to answer you!


✪ If you have scanned any band 2 or 3 times with no reply, try switching bands, and remember to change your scan direction too! Sometimes a spirit can dedicate what the radio is going to pick up before the radio even gets there! I know it sounds impossible, but it is true!


✪ When walking from room to room with your radio, the way you hold it directly affects the reception of the antenna. Keep the unit slightly extended away from your body, and away from other equipment that might be near you. When moving, do so slowly and quietly. Sometimes you might want to fully extend the built in antenna, and often it might work better not extended at all. Depending on your location, you will decide which is best for you and when.

- When doing group Ghost Box sessions, keep the radio in the center of all those who are involved, and keep the volume at a comfortable level, so that you are not over powering any digital voice recorders that may be recording your session. I highly suggest that at least two different voice recorders should be in use during any group sessions. A K2 meter or other EMF device may also be used to confirm any activity, but make sure to keep them a safe distance away from the radio, and be sure to log any EMF spikes on all your recordings for later use.

- If there is more than one person in your investigative group, try giving the Ghost Box to several people, and not just one. Sometimes a spirit will be attracted to one person more than another, or to a particular sex also. If you are getting better responses with one person more than another, make sure to log that information down.

- Your Ghost Box may also be used with a pair of headphones, by plugging them directly into its headphone jack. Some investigators hear things better this way. Personally, I do not like to use them, because it limits what I can hear in the environment. I have also found that sometimes a spirit will like to hear the sound of their voice coming through, and it encourages them to keep speaking with you! Also, understand that depending on the make and model of your particular radio, doing this can disable the built-in speaker, limiting your evidence. Some investigators purposely use headphones in an attempt to drown out what others on their team are talking about, making any answer obtained through the radio associated with the unheard conversation more valid. If you are going to use this method, just make sure you trust the person using the radio. I have seen many teams fake evidence with this process by pretending not to hear questions being asked by other team members. It is unfortunate, but it does happen.

✪     Remember to remain calm! Hearing a voice come through for the first time can be an exciting experience, especially if you are a new, inexperienced investigator. The excitement or fear of you and others will often make the spirit feel as if it has upset you, and it could stop communicating with you. This is a very common occurrence during an investigation, and unfortunately, it really limits the evidence you get. Let your team members know they need to remain calm, and not to say out loud that they are nervous or scared. Fear begets fear!

✪     While the built-in speaker in your radio may sounds great, it still may not be loud enough for everybody to hear it, and turning it up to full volume not only makes it sound over modulated, but it also reduces battery life faster. If this is the case, it is suggested that you purchase a separate pair of auxiliary speakers to plug into the headphone jack. Just make sure that the speakers you use are amplified, and that they run on battery power. An amplified speaker running off its own power causes less interference, uses no battery power from the radio and is completely portable. It does not rely on household power, which as you probably know, is not always available to you in all locations, making it ideal.

## * Recording *

So, you think you have obtained evidence through your Ghost Box, and now are wondering how you can record that evidence for later analysis. Well, the good news is, there are a few different ways you can accomplish this, and I highly suggest recording when doing any Ghost Box session. Sometimes you will be able to understand what you obtained in real time, and sometimes you will only be able to find missed evidence when listening to a recording of your session later. There are typically three ways for you to accomplish this:

## Ambient Recording Method

This is done by simply setting a digital voice recorder next to or in front of, the radio during your session. Most digital voice recorders are extremely sensitive, and will pick up a sound from several feet away, so your recorder does not have to be extremely close. You can also easily hold your recorder in one hand, and operate your Ghost Box in another, to get an adequate recording. I have even placed my recorder around my neck using its stock hand strap post, and a long necklace or leather strap. This is a great method to use when you are moving around a lot, but the recorder does pick up all your movements as well, and that can sometimes muffle out potential evidence, so be warned.

## Direct Recording Method

Very simply put, this is performed by using a length of 1/8th or 3.5mm patch cable, and plugging one end into the radio, and the other end into the microphone port of your voice recorder. You will get nice audio this way, but it does have its drawbacks. For starters, when you use this method, you will notice that unless your voice recorder records in stereo, you will only have recorded audio in one channel; only one ear. Furthermore, plugging anything into the radio's headphone jack automatically disables the built-in speaker on some models, thus you will not be able to hear the responses you get in real time. Some investigators do not care about real time evidence, and some do. You will have to decide if this method of recording is right for you.

## Direct Recording & Monitoring

This method requires you to have a patch cable, and a set of headphones. Basically, you plug your headphones into the headphone port of your digital recorder, and run a patch from your radio's headphone port to your recorder's microphone port.

This will enable you to hear what is being said and record at the same time. Another alternative to headphones is to use auxiliary speakers, like we discussed earlier. Keep in mind that not all voice recorders will perform this function, and this is not a feature most manufactures advertise.

## **Other Recording Methods**

By purchasing a few splitters, and a few patch cables, you can try many different combinations to get the results you are looking for.

For example, if you have a laptop with a headphone port and microphone port, you can utilize these also. Most voice recorders also have these same two ports on them. So, if you were to plug your radio into your voice recorder's microphone port, and then plug your laptop's microphone port into the headphone port on your voice recorder, and start up some type of audio editing software such as Audacity or Adobe Audition, you could in theory, record straight to your laptop's hard drive, and your voice recorder at the same time. In addition, it is possible to use a splitter on a splitter, and convert any port into 2,4 or 6 ports, etc. There are many different possibilities for getting your evidence from your radio recorded, and I suggest you experiment and try them all! Splitters and patch cables can be purchased for very little cost at your local Radio Shack or other retailer.

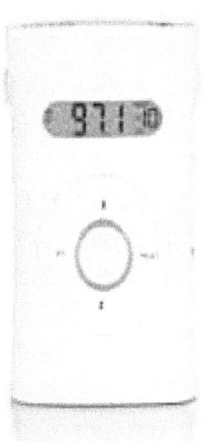

Various Homemade Ghost Boxes For Under $40

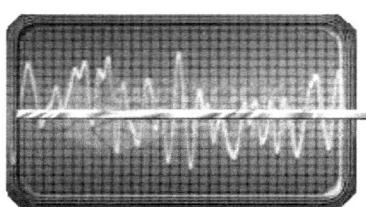

# ~ CHAPTER FIVE ~

## Revewing Your Evidence

The final step, and the most important in the investigative process, is evidence review. Thinking of just simply putting on a set of headphones? It is actually that simple, but like all other steps in the process, there are guidelines. Making sure that you not only catalog your evidence properly, but that your methods remain consistent, is essential. The first thing I will discuss in this chapter is the equipment you will need to use in order to listen, and analyze your recordings.

## **HEADPHONES**

When it comes to listening to audio properly, headphones are a must, and they should be of good quality. Never try to review your evidence without the use of headphones! Obviously, you are not listening to music, so the sound quality does not need to be superb, but your headphones should at least cover the entire human hearing range of 20Hz-20,000Hz. If the headphones you are looking to use do not cover the 20 to 20 range, then do not use them. Most headphones cover the 20 to 20 range, but some cheaper ones, like those found at your local dollar store, do not, and are unsuitable for evidence review. If a potential EVP was recorded at 15,000Hz, and the speakers in your headphones only have a maximum frequency response of 14,000Hz, then you are not going to hear that frequency! Your headphones should also be comfortable to wear for long periods of time. Remember, you are not only going to be reviewing your potential evidence at home, but you could also be reviewing your recordings during the actual investigation while performing burst recording techniques as well, so being comfortable is a must!

There are mainly three different styles of headphones on the market today; ear buds, over the ear, and around the ear. Which one you choose will be up to your individual taste and other personal requirements. Personally, I have two different sets in my equipment bag. I use a set of normal over the ear headphones while on an actual investigation, and I use a set of ear buds for review at home.

When I am on an investigation, I still want to hear subtle things that are going on around me, and at home, I want to eliminate as much background noise as possible, and ear buds that fit right into the ear canal serve this purpose well.

Around the ear styles also work well because they completely surround your entire ear, working better to eliminate unwanted outside noise. The problem with these, however, is that your ears do not get any air circulation, and they can begin to sweat, forcing you to take them off occasionally to let your ears breath.

There are also noise canceling headphones available as well, but ones of good quality, are fairly expensive. These particular headphones work by doing just the opposite of what you would expect; they actually <u>create</u> background noise! By creating background noise, they actually cancel out incoming background noise; a phenomenon known as **Destructive Interference.** The result, is a set of headphones that virtually eliminate outside noise.

While this technology sounds appealing, be careful! Most versions of these headphones can also filter out sounds you want to hear.

These types of headphones are becoming more popular among paranormal investigators, but personally, I do not really see the need to use them. If you are in an environment that is so noisy you cannot review your evidence properly, then you should be doing it in another location. Cancelling out background noises while doing live review could make you miss more evidence. I purchased a set for $20 one time, and I was amazed at how poor the sound quality was compared to the normal set I used. Remember, you get what you pay for when it comes to electronics, and headphones are no exception to the rule! Make sure you use a set that is comfortable, and that covers those frequencies you want to hear!

There are also wireless headphones available, which will simply plug into your computer or voice recorder through a base unit, and then the base unit will send the audio signal wirelessly to the included headphones. Unless the wireless technology that these types of headphones use, utilize high frequencies, you may receive unwanted interference from other devices nearby that use similar frequencies, such as cordless phones, wireless Internet routers and cell phones. These types of headphones also produce a constant level of background noise, which can hinder your ability to properly analysis evidence. Anytime you send an audio signal through the air, it can be influenced by other equipment in the area. So, whenever possible, use a corded set to be safe!

## **Computer Software**

It is not absolutely necessary to review your evidence on a computer with audio editing software, but it sure will make your life a lot easier in the long run, not only for review, but for editing options as well. These types of software programs range from free to very expensive, and while a free utility may sound like the right way to go, it may not have the desired functionality you are looking for. However, in many cases, these free programs will work just fine. The two most popular programs used by most paranormal investigators are Audacity and Adobe Audition.

Audacity is an excellent open source audio recording and editing program that is 100% free, and it works very well. **Open source** simply means that the programming and coding that make up the program is "Open" for anybody to view, change or add to in order to make the program better. The great thing about open-source software, is there are a lot of highly intelligent people behind its success, who would normally be prohibited from providing valuable input by laws and copyright restrictions. Audacity is currently available online for free, and can be found by simply doing a Google search, and downloading it. Several different plug-ins are available, which add more functionality to the program, and several tutorials are also available to those who wish to acquire them.

Your other option is to use Adobe Audition. Adobe has made three different versions of this popular software, with the cheapest being a staggering cost of nearly $300. Choosing to use this software is a personal taste, and it is the software I use. While it is mainly intended for audio professionals, and has many features that will not be used for paranormal investigation, it is still very reliable. It requires no additional plug-in's to run, and has various options that make it a better choice, if you can afford it. If you have watched TAPS or Ghost Lab analyze an EVP on television, then you have seen Adobe Audition at work, and there is a reason they both choose to use it; functionality. It offers not only the ability to record and play audio, but it also allows the user to change certain attributes of a sound file to better enhance different portions of a particular sound. It also allows frequency analysis of any portion of a sound file which I think is essential for EVP work. Adobe Audition used to be called Cool Edit Pro, before Adobe Systems purchased it, and renamed it, but essentially it is still the same exact software, and older versions of Cool Edit Pro are available online for free, if you can find them.

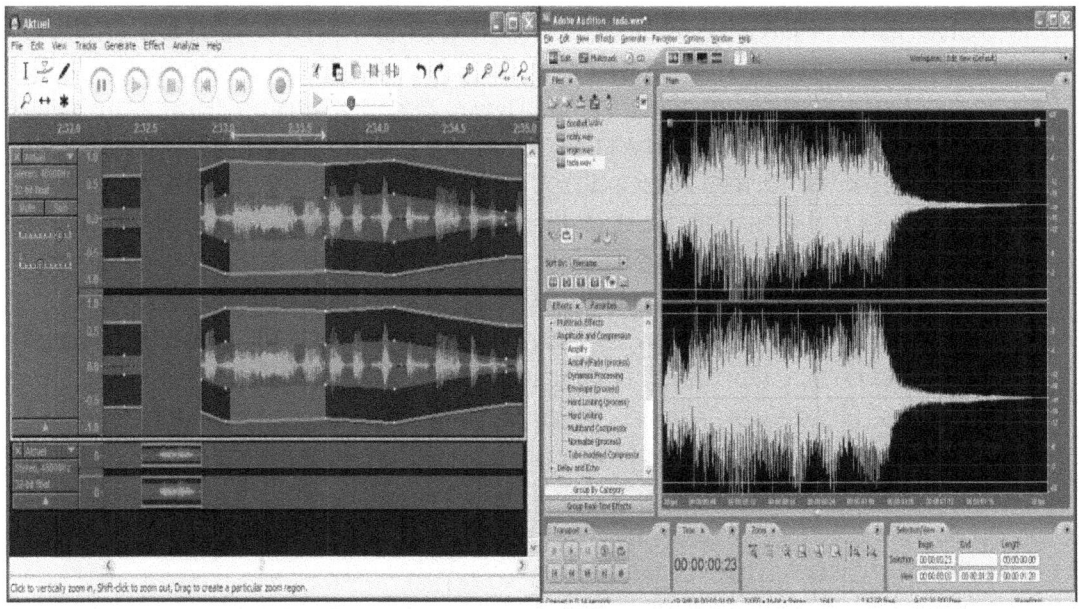

AUDACITY          ADOBE AUDITION

## **Digital Enhancement**

As mentioned above, audio programs like Adobe Audition and Audacity not only offer the ability to play and record sound, but they also offer the ability to clean up, or enhance the audio of any sound file. Often times, you will review your evidence only to find that a potential EVP is being masked by annoying pops, clicks and hissing, or that the recording needs to be made just a little louder.

These problems can all be solved by using sound enhancement filters, and Audacity or Adobe Audition come standard with them, and they are easy features to use. Never apply more than 3 steps of enhancement or filtering to keep your recordings as genuine as possible. The three most widely used filters are:

## •Noise Reduction•

All recording devices have traits which make them susceptible to noise. This noise can be random, and normally manifests as hissing, popping, clicking or white noise introduced by the device's internal mechanism or processing. These annoying sounds can be filtered out by selecting a small part of the recording which contains the strongest noise, and capturing its noise profile. Once this profile has been captured, the software can then determine what type of noise to look for in the recording, and remove it. Not only can it be removed, but it can also be adjusted to a custom level. How much of the noise you want removed is up to you, but take warning, removing too much can ruin your recording! Some software programs offer a preview of how the recording will sound before the noise reduction filter is applied, which makes it easy to spot mistakes. However, some programs do not offer this feature, so always make sure to preview your audio after ANY filter has been applied before saving it, and if you find that the audio sounds worse, just select "Undo" to revert back to the original. Also, never perform noise reduction filtering twice to any part of your sound file, as this can make your recording sound robotic, and some programs will not undo more than 1 step at a time, leaving you to start all over again. If done properly, one step of filtering should be enough to achieve your desired results.

## •Amplify & Fade•

Sometimes you will find that certain parts of your recordings need to be amplified because of low volume, or faded due to over modulation. This is where amplify and fading filters come into play. Just like noise reduction, you can choose the level of filtering to be applied. Again, be sure to check the audio after the filer has been applied for mistakes, before saving. Also, anytime you perform amplification, be sure to do it before you apply any noise reduction. Amplifying the recording can bring unheard noise to the surface, and as mentioned before, you never want to perform noise reduction twice.

## •Time & Pitch•

If you find your possible EVP seems to speak to quickly, making it tough to ascertain what is being said, then the Time/Pitch filter just might benefit you. This can also be called a "Stretch" filter, due to the fact that the recording is actually stretched to be made longer, resulting in slower speech. Sometimes when an EVP is stretched out, it is easier to hear voiced and unvoiced sounds. This should only be done as a temporary filter, in order to enhance clarity, and should never be permanently applied to the final saved version. When it has been determined what is being said, it is important to "Undo" the filter, and revert back to the original for validity.

- **•Always review immediately after each enhancement•**
- **•Never forget to have 2 copies of your audio recording; the original & enhanced versions•**

# REVIEWING TECHNIQUES

Before I can dive into reviewing techniques, there is one important subject to discuss first; **Audible Matrixing** or **Pareidolia.** To better understand Audible Matrixing, you first have to understand **Visual Matrixing**, because they are one in the same.

Remember when you were a child, lying on your back, looking up at the clouds full of wonderment? Ever recall seeing certain shapes and faces in those clouds? Oh look, a spaceship! There goes a lion or an eagle; this is Visual Matrixing. Simply put, it is the mind's way of taking something unfamiliar, and making it familiar. This is how as a child we learned what the difference between a square and a circle was, and without this ability, we would have a hard time as adults even remembering a face. This is also how some psychologists probe deeper in the mind of a patient, by using pictures that resemble many different things, also called **The Rorschach Test**. While this trait is important in brain development, it is even more important when it comes to interpreting paranormal evidence. Just like your mind can make a picture of nothing into a ghost, it can also take a sound that has absolutely no verbal attributes, and turn it into a voice. This is Audible Matrixing.

Have you ever been at a noisy location, such as a cocktail party or Laundromat? It is nearly impossible to ascertain what is being said from across the room with all that loud music or chatter, but as soon as your name is mentioned, you have no problem hearing it.

Audible Matrixing is the mind's way of hearing what it wants, especially if somebody tells you what to listen for. If I put a set of headphones on your ears, and let you listen to a recording of white noise, more than likely that is all you will hear. However, if I tell you that at exactly 10 minutes and 20 seconds into the recording you will hear a male voice say, "Get Out", then there is a high probability you will hear exactly that. This is primarily why one investigator will hear one thing, and others will hear something completely different. It is all a matter of the mind's perception, and how it interprets information.

Of course, there is no fool-proof technique to completely eliminate matrixing, but there are ways to limit its effect, and if you want your evidence to remain pure, you are going to have to learn them. I will discuss these, along with all other reviewing techniques.

- ✓ Review your evidence as soon as possible after the investigation. Weather it is video or audio, you should attempt to review your evidence while the investigation is still fresh in your mind. You could have an important event that was captured, which could merit an immediate return investigation. This is also a courtesy to your client(s) as well.

- ✓ Find a comfortable, quiet, distraction free environment to listen to your audio. Watching the television, listening to the radio, taking a cell phone call or having a review party only adds distraction to an already difficult task.

- ✓ Keep a pen and paper handy. When listening to your audio, if you hear something that sounds like it might be an EVP, do not stop and review, but instead write down the time the event occurred in the recording, and what you thought the voice said or sounded like, then review it later. For example; "#1 evp-male voice whispering10m30s". Try not to immediately review any anomaly, as this can contaminate any proceeding audio by contributing to matrixing.

- ✓ After your initial review, when you are ready to listen to any anomalies you noted down, start with the first one you found, as this will help you avoid matrixing contamination by giving your mind a fresh start in the recording.

- ✓ Remain calm! Capturing an EVP for the first time can be very exciting and overwhelming. Remain calm, and treat it as you would any other form of evidence; with an open mind. Getting your team all worked up over something that may turn out to be nothing, helps nobody. If your evidence actually passes the test, and the majority of the members on your team can agree as to what is being said, then you can celebrate.

- ✓ Never tell another team member what you think is being said. Let every member listen and decide for themselves what they think about the audio, and then you can all share your opinions. If you do not follow this rule, then you are opening yourself up to Matrixing as well as possible future credibility issues. This is the single most important rule to follow when it comes to audio review.

- ✓ Try closing your eyes, or leaving your room poorly lit with just enough light to read and write by. It is a scientifically proven fact, that when one of our senses are impaired, another takes its place. By closing your eyes, you allow your ears to take over, and operate more efficiently. This is why a blind person has super hearing, and a sense of smell that is far superior to that of a normal person.

- ✓ Try to leave your audio as genuine as possible. Many investigators including myself, like to enhance certain EVP's in order to better understand what is being said. While this is not supported by many, I still feel that sometimes it is necessary. If a simple audio amplification enables me to hear a name, then obviously it is worth it. Just do not go too far, and enhance your audio to the point where it is no longer valid. I suggest performing no more that 3 steps of digital enhancement to clean up your audio, and only with class B and below evidence. If you need to perform more than this, then it is not worth your time. Trash it and move on.

- ✓ Take a break. If you have six hours of audio to review, do not try to get it all reviewed in one sitting. Give your mind and ears a rest. If you are having trouble figuring out what something is saying, sometimes taking a break is just the answer.

✓ If you are having a hard time figuring out what is being said, isolate that part of the recording, and listen to it looped. Ever try to remember something, and when you are not thinking about it, bam, the answer comes to you? You can trigger this **Verbal Transformation Effect** by running your audio looped. Listening to a particular section of your audio, and having it repeat may sound stupid, but trust me, it works. What you once thought was something that you were never going to be able to figure out, suddenly becomes clear evidence. Researchers will say to avoid this type of reviewing as it may bring false positives, and contribute to matrixing, but I disagree.

✓ Do not convert your audio files! As we discussed earlier, WAV or PCM format is ideal for audio recording. However, if your particular recorder records in MP3 or WMA, just leave the files that way. Converting to different formats only takes your audio apart and reassembles it into another format, causing possible evidence loss. If you absolutely have to convert, make sure you save your original.

✓ When chopping up your audio files, make sure to save enough audio to make sense of your recording. Do not just save an EVP that says, "Get Out"; make sure you record what came before it, and after. Taking your EVP out of context is considered a sin by most investigators, and will add a lot of confusion when it comes to future review. You do not have to save everything, but if you ask a question, and your question is answered, you obviously will want to make sure you have that question as evidence.

✓ Go with your gut instinct. If you believe in your heart that what you have is "Get Out", and you have tried your best to eliminate matrixing, then go with your instinct. Never let anyone make up your mind for you, or tell you what you have is nothing, especially if you recorded and analyzed it yourself. You definitely need input from others to keep your evidence honest, but do not feel bad if you disagree with them. Your first instinct is usually right.

- ✓ When saving your final cut version of an EVP, always document where in the original recording it was, and where you were, etc. Sure, all this information may be in the original file, but after you pull out that individual EVP, you may no longer have that information, and if you do, it may become lost. I do this by making the file name reflect this information. For example, I will change the file name to:

"GoldfieldHotel/Basement/10.23.2010/30m50s/getout/olympusws700"

....and always save your original versions. If you enhance an EVP, make sure you save your original. I usually have three versions; the entire full recording of the entire session, the chopped out EVP, and the enhanced EVP. Notice I also mentioned what kind of recorder I was using in the file name above. This is important because I frequently use two different types of recorders, and if I want to document which one picked up what, I have that information available to me. Remember, one recorder might pick up an EVP better than another. Most digital voice recorders sold today imprint this information directly onto the file of the recording, but they do not contain enough information about the file for paranormal purposes.

- ✓ Try not to review your evidence on the same recorder you used to capture it. This may be fine for onsite burst recording review, but for final review, it should not be done. Digital voice recorders can be very limiting, and you could miss very subtle hidden attributes. Listening is only a small part of the review process anyway, and using software to view frequency attributes, is a good idea also.

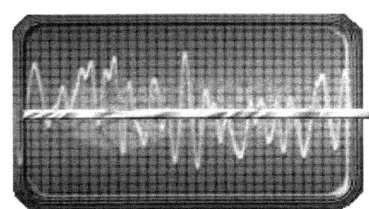

# ~ CHAPTER SIX ~

## Understanding Sound Analysis

This chapter will discuss analyzing EVP and other paranormal sound recordings. Several different analysis methods will be discussed, including waveform and frequency analysis. This chapter will also point out the importance of audio context, automatic gain circuits, and software.

## Listening

Obviously, the way to analyze any sound recording is to listen to it. However, it is also the most subjective method. Scientists have discovered that more of the process of hearing occurs more in the brain than in the ears (audible matrixing). It is crucial to listen to large sections of the recording at any one time so that you become accustomed to the content, particularly the ambient sound levels, or background noise.

Listening to small sections can leave you with false impressions of any anomalies found, which is why in the previous chapter I suggested listening to the entire recording first, making notes of what you heard, and checking for evidence later. It is often difficult to judge what caused a particular noise (like the creaking of a wooden floorboard) unless you go back to the site of the investigation and examine the scene to reproduce it. You may be able to reproduce certain sounds by moving objects around, but this does not necessarily imply that the objects moved paranormally. This is another reason why I suggest using a video recorder, alongside your recorder, as mentioned in an earlier chapter.

Sometimes, we can become convinced of a word or message, even if we are wrong. If words are missed, we often fill in a substitute based on the content. If someone said to you, *"that ball shred"*, you would most likely hear *"that ball is red"*, because it makes more sense. Your mind would substitute 'is' for 'sh' without you even being aware of it, and you would be convinced that you heard it correctly.

You will often find that people disagree about what words are said, when it comes to an EVP. Perhaps the best way to sort this out, is to find a group of friends, preferably people not interested in EVP, and ask them what their opinions are, and then take a vote. I frequently let other people listen to some of my recordings just to get an unbiased opinion. You could also include a few controlled voices in order to keep other's opinions honest. These 'controls' would be ordinary, real voices saying known things. To make them sound more plausible, you could muffle the voice by putting a cloth over the microphone of your recorder. Make sure the clips you play include a few seconds of context on either end of the recording. Most importantly, do not tell your judges what words to expect, as expectations strongly affect results in speech interpretation, paving the road for matrixing.

## Waveforms

How can we know that a certain sound was human speech or that of an EVP? It may seem obvious to most people, but it is a difficult problem for scientists trying to make reliable voice recognition software. Once you have detected speech, there is the hard problem of trying to understand precisely what is being said (everyone's speech sounds slightly different). This is referred to as "The speech Recognition Problem". Are the sounds recorded really voices, and if so, what exactly are they saying?

One characteristic of human speech that is important to understand is **voiced sound**. These are sounds that involve using the larynx, or voice box. If you put your hand over your larynx (at the base of your throat), you can feel it vibrate when you make certain sounds. Sounds, like "s" and "t" are **unvoiced sounds**, as they require only lips and tongue to produce.

Voiced sounds are very common. This is useful to know, because voiced sounds are easily recognizable. The sound our larynx makes is low frequency and very specific. Typically, these sounds are usually at a higher volume than the rest making them even easier to identify. Comparing voiced sounds to unvoiced sounds in your recording, through the use of audio software, will reveal the differences between the two. For example, if you obtained a possible EVP that you think says 'Let Me Out', obviously the 'E' sound in the word 'Let' would be a voiced sound, and the 'T' would be an unvoiced sound. So, what can we use to determine what attributes these different sounds have? We can look at the Waveform of the sound file. **Waveforms** are peak and valley graphs that audio programs use to show us a breakdown of a sound's attributes. Things like specific frequency, length and decibel levels can be studied when viewing waveforms, which is why having audio analysis software, is so important. For example, after looking at the frequency wave or Waveform of a recording, you notice that the voiced part of the speech is the same frequency as the unvoiced section. You could then determine that the recording is not that of typical human speech, as the 2 sections are typically different from one another, as the voiced sounds are typically deeper, at a lower frequency and are higher in volume.

Of course, this does not mean you actually have a legitimate EVP, but it does add credibility...credibility you would not have had without software!

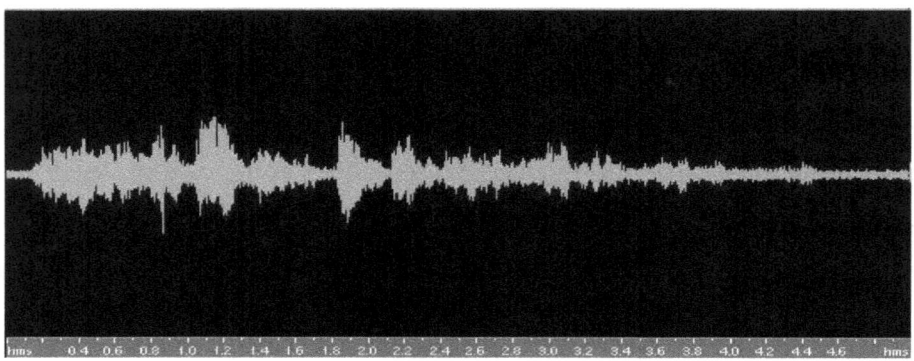

A Typical Sound Waveform In Adobe Audtion

## Phonemes

To better identify human speech, it helps to understand how we form words. All words are a mixture of certain individual sounds called **Phonemes**. Without getting too scientific, and putting it in simple terms, phonemes are the sounds that individual letters make. For example, the word 'Trail' has exactly 4 phonemes. The 'T','R','AI' and 'L' are all phonemes, with the letters 'A' & 'I' making one sound, thus only counting as one. So, what importance do phonemes have when it comes to analyzing our EVP recordings?

Well, by simply breaking down any individual word recorded in a potential EVP into sets of phonemes, we can ascertain if those words have human traits, or if they are paranormal in origin. In a typical human voice, you would be able to listen to each specific phoneme, but all too often with EVP, picking apart these individual sounds is quite difficult as they typically blend together. The phrase should typically sound more like one continuous word than two separate ones, to be a legitimate EVP.

# Frequency Analysis

Another way to determine if a voice you recorded falls into the paranormal category, would be to take a look at its frequency characteristics. While we hear in the 20-20 range as mention earlier, we typically speak in the 100HZ-4,000Hz range. While it is possible for us to speak below and above these ranges, it is not normal, and typically does not happen in normal adult speech. This is obviously important, because if we record a voice at 30HZ, then certainly the potential for it to be paranormal increases. Of course, just because it was recorded below the norm does not mean it is automatically a spirit, but it does send out a red flag for further study. So, how do we analyze a sound and view its frequency?

While this may seem complicated to most, it is actually quite simple. Programs like Audacity and Adobe Audition allow the use of a frequency analysis feature, which will give the specific frequency of any part of your recording. Adobe Audition also incorporates a feature called spectral view, which will assign a specific color to a frequency range, and when you compare these colors to the colors of normal speech, the anomalies pop right out at you. This is a technique that most paranormal investigators use including Ghost Lab and T.A.P.S., so look for it the next time you are watching one of these shows. With the use of waveform and frequency analysis together, you can obtain more insight into the validity of your recordings.

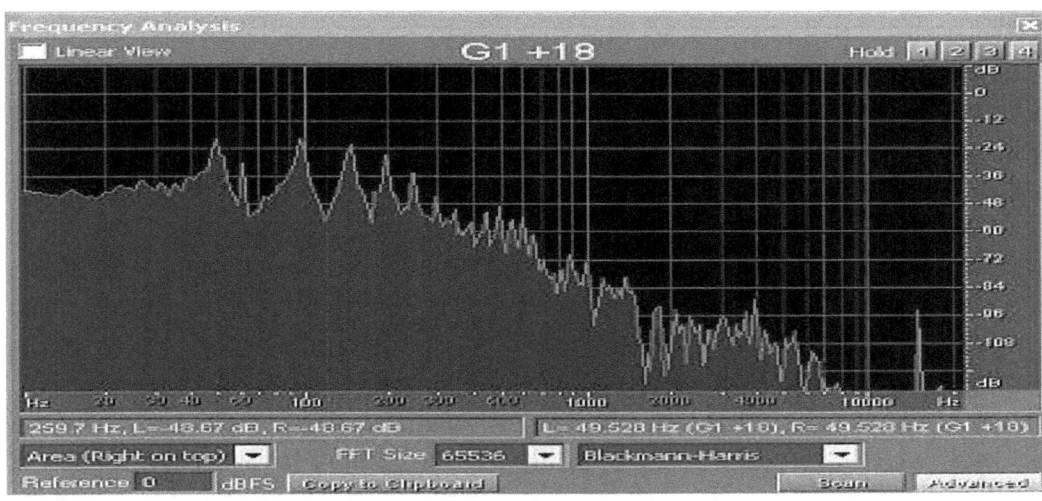

**Adobe Audition Frequency Analysis Screen**

# Background Noise

The use of background noise in your recordings, can sometimes yield the most evidence. All audio recorded, regardless of the type of recording device used, contains some level of background noise. Try turning on your recorder in a perfectly quiet setting, and try recording what you think is silence. After listening to the recording, you will soon find out that silence, is not so silent. A constant level of sound can be heard in the background, and it is this level of background noise, that most researchers say contain the best medium for spirit contact. Of course, the real trick to finding EVP, is determining subtle changes in this level of noise. Doing this requires nothing more than the ability to listen. Pay close attention after any questions asked, or just before any unusual noise is heard. Furthermore, make it a point to seek out, and only listen to background noise for a certain amount of time. Once the mind grows familiar with the level of background noise, subtle differences will stand apart. This is yet another reason why I suggest listening to the entire recording during the initial analysis, as it gives the mind time to adjust to background noise.

Background noise is very important when it comes to recording and analyzing audio. It provides audio context, and reassures the listener that the recording has not been tampered with. It can also provide clues to possible explanations for sounds. For example, is the sound louder than the ambient background noise or about the same level or fainter? If the sound is louder than the background noise, then there is the possibility that it is a real sound that was not noted at the time of recording. It is also possible that the microphone was directional, and aimed at a sound source that no one noticed at the time. Background noise is typically random and unpredictable. If two elements of it (such as a squeaky chair and a creaking floorboard, or an electric fan and a noise from outside) happen to occur at the same time together, they may combine to sound like something unique, and after listening to the background over a long period of time, you may be able to conclude that this is exactly what occurred.

You might think it is impossible to pick up a sound fainter than the background noise, but it does happen. However, if it contains apparent meaningful information, like a voice, it could be audible matrixing. Sometimes you may record sounds from outside the building while you are inside. These may appear to be coming from inside the building, as often there is no easy way of telling from a simple recording where a particular sound originated.

You might even pick up the voice of someone passing the building outside. Remember, as discussed earlier, you should always make note of such details to make analysis easier.

## Auto Gain Control

While listening to your recording, you should be aware if the background noise appears to fade when a loud sound is picked up. This could mean that your recorder has an **Auto-Gain Control** or AGC. It is the AGC's job to keep sound levels roughly constant or normalized. Most voice recorders have an AGC, and since most recorders are made just for dictation purposes, they do not advertise this feature, and it cannot be turned off. The AGC turns the microphone sensitivity to high during quiet periods (amplifying background noise), and low during noisy ones (when the background fades away). This can make it very difficult to judge the loudness of different sound sources within the recording.

It also tends to amplify background noise, which can produce false positives. In addition, the AGC also affects the very part of the recorder that is most susceptible to radio interference; the microphone. The AGC can give normal recordings a strange sound, and the way in which the background sound can vanish and re-appear, can be quite confusing.

Unfortunately, it is just normal operation for the AGC which is designed primarily for applications where there are not long silent periods. The only good thing about the AGC, is that if it reacts to a sound, it means the sound is real and fairly loud, which is useful information to have.

Some people deliberately ask questions very loud to elicit EVP, and they leave an extra long silent gap for the answer before asking the next question. If the recorder has an AGC, it will tend to amplify the bits between the questions making an answer more prominent.

Automatic gain circuits are common in most voice recorders however, if you can get hold of a recorder with manual controls, so that you can override AGC, it would make life easier. I have seen such equipment sold today, but unfortunately, the prices are high, and the recorders are extremely large, not making them very portable.

## 10 General EVP Traits
## Courtesy of the AAEVP

1. **Distinctive:** EVP often have a specific timing, pitch, frequency, volume and use of background sound. The voices have a very selective sound that is tough to describe. EVP messages often have words that seem to be spoken faster than human speech with subtle pauses between words. You may also notice that voices often have a hollow sound quality.

2. **Frequency Range:** EVP are sometimes received at higher or lower frequencies than normal speech.

3. **Precursor Sounds:** Quite often, sounds are heard prior to an EVP, and tend to be within tenths of a second of a phrase, and resemble a "popping" or "clicking" noise. Much study is currently being conducted in an attempt to understand why these sounds exist. One explanation that I have concluded, is that these sounds are the result of different levels of immeasurable energy being released into the environment, directly affecting the recording device.

4. **Limited Available Energy:** It is believed by some researchers that the quality of EVP is directly related to the energy that is used. A short EVP will tend to be louder than a long EVP. In addition, a sound may suddenly stop or become faint at the end, as if the energy is being used up or discharged before the message is completed. Supporting evidence is very strong that EVP are only as strong as the energy that is used to create them.

5. **Complete Phrases:** An EVP message is normally one to two seconds long, and specific words are usually complete, even when fading. If EVP were crosstalk, like some suggest, then they would begin in the middle of a word. EVP messages are usually complete thoughts, as well.

6. **Language of the Investigator:** It is normal for an EVP, no matter where it was recorded, to be in the same language that the investigator normally speaks. Numerous tests have also been done where the investigator speaks several different languages, but the EVP will come through speaking the language the investigator uses the most or is the most fluent in.

7. **Not Ambient Sound or Radio Broadcasts:** EVP have been recorded and tested in chambers that were shielded from Radio Frequency (RF), such as those designed by the military. This has been clearly demonstrated to prove that EVP are not stray sounds or RF as skeptics would have us believe.

8. **Direct Responses:** Many types of EVP are clearly direct responses to questions asked at the time of recording.

9. **Voices Often Recognizable:** It is common for an EVP to have many recognizable attributes of the entity communicating.

10.  **Speaking**: It is also normal for any entity to say a word or phrase in the same manner while they were alive…their personality clearly carries over with them.

# Judging Your Evidence

So, you have analyzed your audio, and you have taken a close look at the frequency it was recorded in. You have also devoted close attention to background noise, and been on the lookout for voiced and non-voiced sounds. You have broken the sound down into Phonemes, and looked for any normal human attributes. You have done everything to try and disprove the EVP with any factual evidence obtained. So, where does the final decision to classify the EVP as paranormal come from? Ultimately, the decision comes from you, and you alone! You are the final word when it comes to defining what is paranormal, and what is not, and your reputation depends on analysis. If the recording you obtained could not be classified as paranormal, then what was it that you recorded? Again, this is something that you must decide.

There are dozens of possibilities that might explain EVP. Many skeptics suggest that everything from stray radio waves, to solar flare activity is responsible. They of course could be correct, but proving that is as difficult as proving they are legitimate. My point here, is that there are no definite answers, and no set of official rules to follow. The paranormal is very subjective, and ultimately, you must provide your own answers, through investigation, and research. The best advice I can give when it comes to audio evidence, is to keep an open mind, and look at your evidence dispassionately. Follow the guidelines written in this book, and stay true to yourself. Remember, until we can prove why a specific EVP was recorded, they will remain paranormal, so do not be afraid of this classification.

# CONCLUSION

EVP gathering and analysis, is just one of many fundamental aspects of paranormal investigation. The main evidence you can expect to obtain from your many future investigations is audio, and therefore, no other form of evidence can yield more importance.

I hope you have learned that to become proficient, it takes dedication, patience and perseverance. It is no television show out there, and those who strive to find their own personal answers, have to be willing to go the extra mile. In short, it simply means staying true to yourself. As a paranormal investigator, your local community is watching you, and if you are posting evidence online, then the Internet is watching you as well. We can help those afflicted, donate our time to our local communities, put on conferences with no notoriety, but the second we drop the ball, and have our evidence debunked, it seems the whole world looks at us like corrupt politicians.

Hopefully, you have learned much from the information in this book. However, the most valuable information will come from personal experience in the field, and with this experience, also comes responsibility. Many investigators are in this field of study for the wrong reasons; fame and monetary gain. It is my personal hope, that those of you new to paranormal investigation stay true to yourselves and to the paranormal communities you represent. It is also my hope, that one day all investigators will come together to share evidence instead of competing for it.

Stay true, be responsible with your evidence, and go the extra mile to keep your investigations genuine. You represent not only yourself, but all investigators in this field as well. While EVP has a long history of study, we are no closer to understanding its true origins, nor are we able to reproduce it at will. Skeptics will say it is just a stray radio signal, the internal sounds generated by the recorders themselves, and even our own minds trying to understand sounds that are not there. While the above explanations lend credibility, they still do not explain why we are able to ask a direct question, and get a direct response. Explain why in a sealed room free from all **RF** (radio frequency), we still record a mysterious voice. Even help us to understand why when we enter a paranormal location, our recorders suddenly turn off.

Perhaps we may never be able to explain why these mysterious sounds and events occur, but one thing is for sure, the popularity of Electronic Voice Phenomena continues to grow every year. No matter how many tell us what we are doing is a waste of time, one fact ultimately remains; until these skeptics can prove with absolute certainty that EVP is something <u>normal</u>, it will remain <u>paranormal</u>.

# GLOSSARY OF TERMS

## Anomaly

Any occurrence or object that is strange, unusual or unique.

## Matrixing/Pareidolia

The human trait of looking for the familiar in the unfamiliar. Associated with audio and visual, and can be triggered by outside stimulus.

## Auto Gain Control

An adaptive electronic system found in many electronic audio devices used specifically for normalizing sounds, which occur at different levels of intensity and volume.

## A.V.P. (Audible Voice Phenomena)

A disembodied audible anomaly captured on more than one electronic recording device, which is heard in the live environment at the time of capture, and resembles a human voice.

## Disembodied

Evidence lacking in substance, solidity or any firm relation to reality.

## E.V.P. (Electronic Voice Phenomena)

A disembodied audible anomaly captured on any electronic recording device, which resembles a human voice.

## Frequency Response

The measure of any output in response to an input signal.

### I.T.C. (Instrumental Trans-Communication)

Attempted communication through any sort of electronic device such as tape recorders, fax machines, television sets or computers between spirits or other discarnate entities and the living.

### Intelligent Evidence

Events that are unique to a specific situation, often react and reply to direct questioning or stimulus, and are associated with other events such as sudden temperature changes, EMF spikes, smells or odors, object manipulation and manifestations.

### L.E.D. (Light Emitting Diode)

A semiconductor device that emits infrared or visible light when charged with an electric current. These will eventually replace all standard incandescent filament type light bulbs because of their ability to create light with very little heat, and run efficiently without fail for up to 100,000 hours before replacement is needed.

### Li-ion (Lithium Ion)

Family of rechargeable battery types in which lithium ions move from the negative electrode to the positive electrode during discharge, and back when charging. They are one of the most popular types of rechargeable battery for portable electronics, with one of the best energy densities, no memory effects, and a slow loss of charge when not in use. Beyond consumer electronics, they are also growing in popularity for military, electric vehicle, and aerospace applications.

## Lossy Audio

A data encoding method which compresses data by discarding (losing) some of it. The procedure aims to minimize the amount of data that needs to be held and/or transmitted by a computer, or other audio/video device.

## Manifestation

One of the forms in which someone or something, such as a person, a divine being or idea is revealed.

## M.P.E.G. (Motion Picture Experts Group)

A working group of experts who were formed in 1988 to set standards for audio and video compression/transmission.

## MP3 (MPEG Layer Three)

A patented digital audio encoding format using a form of lossy data compression. It's a common audio format for consumer audio storage, as well as a popular standard of digital audio compression for the transfer and playback of music on digital audio players.

## NiCad (Nickel Cadmium Battery)

A type of rechargeable battery using nickel oxide hydroxide and metallic cadmium as electrodes. Popular for many years, this type of battery is now considered ancient but is still widely used for portable electronic devices. This type of battery has low capacity and high rate of self discharge, often called "Memory Effect".

## NiMH (Nickel-Metal Hydride Battery)

A type of rechargeable battery similar to the nickel-cadmium cell. The NiMH battery uses a hydrogen-absorbing alloy for the negative electrode instead of cadmium. A NiMH battery can have two to three times the capacity of an equivalent size nickel-cadmium battery. Compared to the lithium-ion cell, the energy is similar but self-discharge is higher. Currently, the most widely used type of rechargeable battery.

### Occam's Razor

A scientific precept which states that all things being equal, the simplest explanation is usually the correct one.

### Paranormal

A general term that designates outside "The range of normal experience or scientific explanation", or that indicates phenomena that are understood to be outside of science's current ability to explain or measure.

### Phonemes

The individual sounds that make up human speech. Not only is each letter of the alphabet technically a Phoneme, but combinations of certain letters together are as well.

### Residual Evidence

Events trapped in time that seem to repeat themselves over and over, may have weak strength, and often don't relate or react to any specific question, stimulus or situation. Moreover, known as "Environmental Imprinting".

### S.R.P. (Selective Recording Phenomena)

A situation when multiple audio recording devices are used to record a specific event at the same time, but only one device is successful.

### Sticky-Shed Syndrome

A condition created by the deterioration of the binders in a magnetic tape, which hold the iron oxide magnetic coating to its plastic carrier. This deterioration renders the tape unusable. Known causes include the absorption of moisture, tape stretch, dust and old age.

## Transform E.V.P.

EVP formation using the transformation of available audio-frequency energy into voice, which is thought to occur in the electronic equipment. Transform EVP was traditionally accomplished by using radio static (white noise) as background sound. Current practices involve the use of unmodulated noise, such as that produced by a fan or other electromagnetic device.

## Unvoiced Sound

Human speech or sounds that are made using just the lips, teeth and tip of the tongue, requiring no use of vocal cords.

## Verbal Transformation Effect

An effect created by listening to something unfamiliar repeatedly until something recognizable is heard. Closely related to audible matrixing, but without the suggested stimuli. While frowned on by investigators, it is still a valuable tool often used in audio analysis. Often, the brain will need to hear something more than once in order to ascertain its content.

## Voiced Sound

Human speech or sounds that can't be made without the use of vocal cords.

## V.O.R. (Voice Operated Recording)

The use of a special feature set in most digital recording devices, where the recording process is automatically started after sensing any ambient sound.

## Waveform

The shape and form of a signal, such as a sound moving in a physical medium. An easy way to think of waveform sound is to picture a wave on the ocean. The ocean is the sound, and the wave is a specific frequency is which the sound travels, having a certain height and speed.

## White Noise

A type of noise that is produced by combining sounds of all different frequencies together. If you took all the imaginable tones that a human can hear, and combined them together, you would have white noise.

# Notes:

# Notes:

# Notes:

# Voices From Beyond
## Victor S. Mannahan, CPI

In Cooperation With:

www.silverstateparanormal.org

www.ingramcontent.com/pod-product-compliance
Lightning Source LLC
Chambersburg PA
CBHW080446110426
42743CB00016B/3296